Sunday's
WORD

BISHOP JOHN HEAPS

HOMILIES FOR YEAR A
Sunday's WORD

First published in 1995 by
E.J. Dwyer (Australia) Pty Ltd
Unit 13, Perry Park
33 Maddox Street
Alexandria NSW 2015
Australia
Ph: (02) 550 2355
Fax: (02) 519 3218

Copyright © 1995 John Heaps

This book is copyright. Apart from any fair dealing for the purposes of private study, research, criticism or review, as permitted under the Copyright Act, no part may be reproduced by any process without written permission. Inquiries should be addressed to the publisher.

National Library of Australia
Cataloguing-in-Publication data

>   Heaps, John E., 1927– .
>   Sunday's Word : homilies for year A.
>
>   ISBN 0 85574 222 4.
>
>   1. Catholic Church – Sermons. 2. Church year sermons.
>   3. Sermons, Australian. I. Title.
>
>   252.6

Cover design by Megan Smith
Text design by Megan Smith
Typeset in Adobe Bembo 12/14.5 pt by Egan-Reid Ltd
Printed in Australia by Alken Press Pty Ltd, Smithfield

10 9 8 7 6 5 4 3 2 1
99 98 97 96 95

Distributed in the United States by:
  Morehouse Publishing
  871 Ethan Allen Highway
  RIDGEFIELD CT 06877
  Ph: (203) 431 3927
  Fax: (203) 431 3964

Distributed in Canada by:
  Meakin and Associates
  Unit 17
  81 Auriga Drive
  NEPEAN, ONT K2E 7Y5
  Ph: (613) 226 4381
  Fax: (613) 226 1687

Distributed in Ireland and the UK by:
  Columba Book Service
  93 The Rise
  Mount Merrion
  BLACKROCK CO. DUBLIN
  Ph: (01) 283 2954
  Fax: (01) 288 3770

Distributed in New Zealand by:
  Catholic Supplies (NZ) Ltd
  80 Adelaide Road
  WELLINGTON
  Ph: (04) 384 3665
  Fax: (04) 384 3663

Dedicated
to
*Cecilia Martin, Jocelyn Kramer and
George Rummery and to the others
whose affirmation over the years
has been both encouragement and
challenge to preach the Gospel.*

With thanks
to

*Win Childs without whom these
words would not be on these pages.*

"Lord, who can grasp all the wealth of just one of your words? What we understand is much less than what we leave behind, like thirsty people who drink from a fountain. For your word, Lord, has many shades of meaning just as those who study it have many different points of view. The Lord has colored his word with many hues so that each person who studies it can see in it what he loves. He has hidden many treasures in his word so that each of us is enriched as we meditate on it."

From St Ephraem's Commentary on the Diatessaron.

Please read the Scripture for the Mass of the day. Then read these homilies in the spirit of the words given.

Where there is no reference given for a quotation, it is from the readings of the day.

Contents

Sundays of Advent
- First — *9*
- Second — *11*
- Third — *13*
- Fourth — *15*

Midnight Mass Christmas — *17*
Feast of the Holy Family — *19*
The Epiphany — *21*
The Baptism of the Lord — *23*

Sundays of Lent
- First — *25*
- Second — *28*
- Third — *30*
- Fourth — *32*
- Fifth — *34*

Passion Sunday — *36*
Easter Sunday — *38*

Sundays of Easter Time
- Second — *40*
- Third — *42*
- Fourth — *44*
- Fifth — *46*
- Sixth — *48*
- Seventh — *50*

The Ascension of the Lord — *52*
Pentecost Sunday — *54*
Trinity Sunday — *56*
The Body and Blood of Christ — *58*

The Assumption of the Blessed Virgin Mary — *60*

Sundays of Ordinary Time

- Second — 62
- Third — 64
- Fourth — 66
- Fifth — 68
- Sixth — 70
- Seventh — 72
- Eighth — 74
- Ninth — 76
- Tenth — 78
- Eleventh — 80
- Twelth — 82
- Thirteenth — 84
- Fourteenth — 86
- Fifteenth — 88
- Sixteenth — 90
- Seventeenth — 92
- Eighteenth — 94
- Nineteenth — 96
- Twentieth — 98
- Twenty-first — 100
- Twenty-second — 102
- Twenty-third — 104
- Twenty-fourth — 107
- Twenty-fifth — 109
- Twenty-sixth — 111
- Twenty-seventh — 113
- Twenty-eighth — 115
- Twenty-ninth — 117
- Thirtieth — 119
- Thirty-first — 121
- Thirty-second — 123
- Thirty-third — 125

The Feast of Christ the King — 127

First Sunday of Advent

". . . they suspected nothing until the Flood came and swept all away. It will be like this when the Son of Man comes." "This is the good news of the Lord!"

So that is good news?

In fact it is. Consider who is saying these things and the love that causes such urgency of feeling.

During Advent the Church invites us to a deep consideration of the wonder of God among us, God one of us, God within us.

What wonderful news that God's love pursues us to the point of his becoming one of us. It is always good news when disaster is avoided through heeding a warning to wake up. "So stay awake because you do not know the day when your master is coming." "You must wake up now."

This being alert is not being afraid or on edge. It is being aware. Only by being in touch with God, with myself and with others can I be aware of the things that really matter. God's message is a gift. But like many other gifts, to be of any value to us it has to be graciously received and valued. Jesus tells us to grasp the great reality of his coming, to ponder it, treasure it and live by its message.

It is a waste when opportunity comes and we miss it by laziness or distraction with trivia.

So as not to waste the wonder of Christmas the Church

gives us Advent as a time to ponder in prayer the event to come.

"The Son of Man is coming at an hour you do not expect." When we live in the presence of the Son of Man we are more likely to recognize him as he comes to us in so many ways and in so many people this week and throughout our lives. For this, too, is his advent. "I tell you solemnly, insofar as you did this to one of the least of these brothers of mine, you did it to me" (Mat 25:40). The disciple with the heart and mind of Jesus will hardly miss the coming of his Lord.

For a person who has lived an Advent life, the final coming, expected or unexpected, will be total joy. Such people will recognize fully the one they have recognized through a glass, darkly. The prophet has invited, "let us walk in the light of the Lord." The light in which we have walked will be, in the final advent, a brilliance illuminating total love and total happiness.

Second Sunday of Advent

The bold words of St Matthew put these Advent characters in stark contrast. John the Baptist, the man of integrity who makes way for the man of ultimate integrity; and the Pharisees and Sadducees, the people of power through manipulation and expediency.

On the one hand, John the Baptist, who held great power and influence with the people, exercised his power for freedom. He saw what he possessed as part of the great picture of liberation for his people. He had a part to play in the revelation of the Redeemer. He was willing to do all he could to work towards truth and to step aside for one greater than himself. Soon he would be in prison. Soon he would be killed because of his commitment to truth.

On the other hand, the Pharisees and Sadducees would, throughout Matthew's Gospel, show themselves to be what John saw in them that day by the Jordan. He saw through the pretence of their "coming for baptism." They came because their power and authority was threatened. When Jesus, "unlike the scribes, taught with authority" (Mk 1:22) he was even more of a threat. They later compromised, made deals together, plotted and lied to remove this threat to their power. Here on this day they fell back on the escape common to narrow-minded, self-sufficient people: "We have Abraham for our Father." This echoes through the utterances of all the master races and colonizers and super human egotists who place themselves above others because of race and so-called breeding and class or presumed superior inherent intelligence. "God can raise up children of Abraham from these stones" was John's reply to such stupidity. Yet he still invited them to repent, to listen and to change.

That was John's mission: to prepare people to listen to the one who would follow him. The voice in the wilderness prepared us to listen to the Lord.

This sublime Advent character speaks to us today. All of us need to listen. We need to approach Advent and this very day, this week, life itself, with listening hearts. There are those who say in some way or other, "we are children of Abraham, we have nothing to learn." This unfortunate state can possess a person of any age. Such people need the spirit of the strong man of the desert who is big enough to look at himself, stripped of all props in the wilderness. He is strong enough to accept his call and all that it implies: the greatness and courage and all the limitations of who he is. He has great gifts but ultimately his gifts have meaning only in relation to God and in relation to the one who precedes him in eternity and follows him in time. John's gift was to know this.

Third Sunday of Advent

In the third chapter of St Matthew's Gospel we hear St John the Baptist acknowledging Jesus: "I should be baptized by you, yet you come to me" (Mat 3:14). We are told of the spirit of God and the voice from heaven acknowledging Jesus in the presence of John, "This is my beloved son. My favor rests on him" (Mat 3:17).

Yet here in Chapter 11 John is sending his disciples to ask the question, "Are you the one who is to come?"

What thoughts came to John in the dark silence of prison? Perhaps they are the thoughts that troubled the disciples and trouble disciples and prospective disciples still.

Where is God's power to bring the evil into line? Why is one who loves him and waits upon his will in prison at the whim of a selfish, proud man? Where is the refining fire that was promised?

Jesus gave an answer to John's disciples. Evil will be overcome by good—persistent, slow, persevering good. God's presence is there touching those who wish to come into its contact. They hear, they see, they walk freely, the lepers are touched and are no longer outcasts. Life is given. The poor matter. It is a coming of the kingdom, not by flashes of mighty power, destroying instantly the evil and anointing the good with worldly power. God's way in nature is the way of gradual growth and change. We patiently wait for the rain and for the sun, each in its own way to give life. God's perfection of nature is also through the patient progress of goodness dispensed through his creatures.

Matthew has revealed a Savior—God who is gentle and gently appeals to our love. Here, then, Jesus points to the signs. They are not signs of punishment and destruction, but signs of care, love and hope, particularly to those rejected by the powerful of the world. Happy is the one who does not lose faith in this caring, loving God who calls us into his life so that we, in our own way, measure and capacity, can be the same. Only in this way will the sign continue to be present for those who choose to see.

Then from Jesus came this beautiful affirmation of John, the faithful one who is in prison because he is faithful to the truth. The gentleness God calls for is certainly not weakness. It is not the reed bowing to every human opinion simply to be popular. It is not the softness of self-indulgence that distracts from the needs of others: the softness represented here by the fine clothes of the Pharisees. It is the healing gentleness of the prophet who sees that only in a kingdom of justice can charity have true meaning.

John has responded to the call of greatness by being who he is: that is, by being humble. God has been able to raise him to greatness because all he wanted was to be no other, to seem to be no other, than God's instrument. He is there if he is needed, he steps aside for someone infinitely greater.

Fourth Sunday of Advent

"I am my own person; do things in my own way." There is even a song about it mostly sung with apparent self-satisfaction and self-centered pride.

In one sense there is only one way we can do things. We can only do anything using our own precious and limited gifts. But if we mean by "I did it my way" that I resented advice or treated the opinion of others with contempt then I am likely to be a menace.

People who see only their own point of view and who must justify their every decision and action as the only way, wreak havoc. How many relationships have been destroyed, children made miserable, parents despondent, peoples even brought to war by narrow-minded, self-righteous people?

Ahaz, the man in the first reading, did it his way in this sense. Through the prophet God was assuring Ahaz that he could trust in the Lord and did not have to turn to foreign alliances. For the king it was too much of a risk. He would rather trust the weapons of war that he can see than the God he cannot see. It is an old story repeated over and over to our shame and loss. Wrong remedies often fix things quickly but, being wrong, cause long-term loss and evil. Sin solves nothing either on the personal level or on the national or international level.

The story presented in today's Gospel looks, for a while, as though it may go the same way. Joseph can't see what these mysterious events have to do with his life. He decides to go his own way—to do it his way. He will get out while the going is good. As with Ahaz, God calls him to change his mind. Joseph listens, considers, sees there is another way and changes.

Joseph certainly does it his way. But his way becomes truly his after he has listened, prayed, talked, changed and decided that this is best. It may not be the most comfortable life, but it is according to truth.

Thus, through the co-operation of Joseph, Jesus is, according to law, the son of Joseph, therefore of the House of David—Joseph's tribe. The prophesies are fulfilled. Jesus is the Son of God—descended of David.

The Almighty has allowed his plan to depend on human co-operation. He has and still does invite us into it. We will enjoy his kingdom forever. God invites us to be part of its company here and now.

Mary and Joseph are our examples of working with the divine plan. They are available to God. They pray, listen, talk, think and then decide to do what seems to be God's will. Then they accept all that that implies by way of trouble, sorrow, joy and fulfillment.

Midnight Mass Christmas

This scene, reenacted throughout the ages, captures our imagination and entrances the spirit of the child within us. The King of Kings and Lord of Lords to whom we sing alleluia is found by shepherds wrapped in swaddling clothes and lying in a manger. But like many heroic acts and idealized deeds, the greatness was not in the physical beauty but in the spirit which inspired and gave life and meaning to the deed.

What we have idealized here in the Christmas scene was actually physical deprivation and hardship brought about by the will of a foreign power far away and by circumstances and people close by. This is part of life. Jesus enters human life, so like any human being the will of others has its effect for happiness and sorrow, comfort and discomfort. The poorer one is and the less politically influential, the more one is at risk.

Christmas challenges this.

The poor shepherds, way down on the financial, political and social scale, are terrified by an outside power coming into their lives. They are soon reassured. It is the power of the creative, loving God. "Do not be afraid. Listen." St Luke, so insistent on good news to the poor, has the poor as stars of the scene. For them it is good news. The Savior has come at last and he is one of them. He is to be found in a manger. They are invited to go to a manger, a place in which they will feel comfortable, at home, to people who will accept them and even listen to them.

The whole scheme of things is turned around. Caesar Augustus, Herod, the High Priest know nothing about this. If they care, eventually, to listen to people like poor shepherds they will come to know perhaps that it is too much to ask of people conscious of their perceived intellectual, political, social and financial superiority.

"Christmas is for children." We hear it every year. The sentimental myth of Christmas is for the childish. The deep spiritual beauty and challenge is for people mature enough to become like little children and to look and listen and wonder at the mystery and value of every human being, and to learn. Christmas invites us all to see beyond the walls that prejudice has constructed and to look at the wonder God has created.

The statement is made quite clearly in this Gospel scene. God is with us, calling us to break down the barriers and let love flow. Only when we do this will we become what he has become for us. Only then, when we are liberated from the destructive power of sin, will the creative power of the Christmas message be good news for all.

The good news is announced in graphic terms. God became one of us so that we may become one with him. We are able to become one with him by living as Jesus lived, thus accepting the divine and eternal life he offers! Living this life implies a likeness to God who is creator and lover of all his children without distinction. It is to this maturity that Christmas invites. God's gift is himself.

Feast of the Holy Family

Immediately after Christmas we are called to reflect on and honor Jesus with the people through whom God chose to give him human life, love, care and nourishment. With Mary's "be it done to me as you will" God has entered our world as one of us. With the humble acceptance of Joseph as "he took his wife to his home" a place where Jesus would grow to maturity was established. As we see the comings and goings of the Holy Family both before and after the birth of Jesus we see that this place had little to do with any specific location. It had everything to do with the things we celebrate today.

If any one word comes to me from today's liturgy of the word it is "respect."

For this reason I present the feast of the Holy Family to all, whether we are man or woman, boy or girl, married or single.

The gentle message of respect for parents in the first reading has nothing to do with whether they are useful or presentable or even mentally capable. They are God's creation and his instruments of our creation. St Paul is realistic when he calls children to be obedient. But he is also realistic when he calls parents to live and act in such a way to deserve obedience and respect.

There are times when obedience to conscience and so to God calls us to go beyond the ties of natural affinity. Later in his life Jesus is to warn his followers that loyalty to the truth, to God, goes beyond all other loyalties. But compassion, kindness and humility, gentleness and patience, bearing with one another, ready forgiveness are all founded on respect for the other. They will lead to God's will and our ways being the same.

No matter who we are, we all have relationships with our fellow human beings. Therefore we are all called to respect God's creations, whoever they are.

Both first and second readings are products of their time. The earthly reward of long life for parental respect was offered in the book of Ecclesiasticus. St Paul's advice for wives to give way to their husbands, too, is a product of its time.

But Jesus takes us beyond these things. He went down to Nazareth and was obedient to them but was not rewarded with long life. He shares his vision, his knowledge of our ultimate destiny, with us. There is something greater than long life and earthly prosperity. So also with his Gospel message. It is ultimately to God that both Joseph and Mary are loyal and obedient. When they learn it is God who calls them to get up and go, this they do even at their own inconvenience. When we are in tune with creation we know that the small picture of our life and relationships is part of the great canvas.

The Epiphany

From the beginning of his life Jesus began to disturb people. If we think Christmas is just about a sweet inner glow and a time to drop the diet and indulge ourselves a little, well just keep reading the Gospels for a few more verses. Christmas is a call for us to grow up and become like little children.

The feast of the Epiphany calls us to open our minds to the mind of Jesus and open our hearts to put them in time with the beat of the heart of Jesus. I once read a letter to a newspaper that was written by a child who had friends of different ethnic backgrounds and who wondered why people developed into racists as they grew older.

The Epiphany is the celebration of God's universal love. It is his statement that God has no favorites. "It means that pagans now share the same inheritance, that they are part of the same body, and that the same promise has been made to them, in Christ Jesus through the Gospel."

No wonder Herod is perturbed—"and so was the whole of Jerusalem." Foreigners came trying to tell them about the Messiah. Wise men from the east. What would they know. Pagans! However, it was best for Herod to be on the safe side. If there were a threat to his power he would trace it down and be rid of it.

For Herod there was no question of wondering whether he might find the truth if he followed the star. He was safe and content as he was.

The challenge of the Epiphany is the call of God for us to move from where we are and to follow the star to the place where Mary and Joseph present us with Jesus. He is not in the palaces of kings or the houses of the rich and worldly powerful but in the place of the poor and unaccepted. He is not in the safety of his own home or even in a country at peace with itself. He is in Bethlehem because of a foreign power and the will of its emperor. His country is occupied by an unwelcome pagan empire. Yet we are to see him later in life even to reach out to these "enemies" in gestures of kindness reflecting the universal love printed here in St Matthew's Gospel.

In this feast Jesus reaches out to the whole world with the message of God's universal love. He invites us to become his followers in deep spirit and truth. He invites us into an intimate relationship with the God of universal love.

But he warned, to love God with mind and soul and heart involves the risk and adventure in the journey out to love our neighbor as ourselves. The message of the Epiphany is disturbing but sublime.

The Baptism of the Lord

By God's creative act the wonder of life and spirit, that which we call soul, and the elements of the earth, that which we call matter, meet in human nature. Now, by God's gift of Jesus, this wonder, called human being, is not only the union of spirit and matter but the union of creature and creator. In one person human and divine nature are united.

We know from the Gospel that Jesus grew in wisdom, stature and favor with God and man. This took place in the quiet obscurity of his home with Mary and Joseph in Nazareth. All the while that wondrous union existed. God walked with us in an entirely new way. Now the time has come for the story of God's extraordinary love to be told. The revelation of what we are to God and his gift to us is to be made. Jesus is about to invite us into the union of God and humanity that he has established.

Here, by the Jordan, he mingles with his fellow human beings. He is one with them in all things but sin. But he still immerses himself in their condition. Although innocent he accepts the consequences of sin.

The human condition is brought about on the one hand by God's love and on the other by our sinfulness. That goodness, love, justice and peace can be regained by the unselfish acts of admitting wrong, asking pardon, repentance. Then the forgiven begin to become forgivers themselves. By God's grace the redeemed take part in the redemption.

Sunday's Word

His immersion in the Jordan is a sign that Jesus immerses himself in our lives, our joys and sorrows and troubles. He will never stand aloof even to the point of being misunderstood, neglected and killed. "He will neither waver nor be crushed until true justice is established on earth." However, he will invite and encourage, never destroy. "He does not break the crushed seed nor quench the wavering flame."

John the Baptist sees the wonder of God present among his people: "It is I who need baptism from you." The integrity, the faithfulness, the love is sealed by the voice from heaven. "This is my son, the Beloved, my favor rests on him."

Immersed in Jesus, we carry God's love and favor into our time and place.

First Sunday of Lent

Millions of people have heard or heard about the stories told today. Probably many more would know of the garden of Eden than the temptation of Jesus in the desert.

With regard to Eden, some have got bogged down with gardens and fruit and whether it is fact or fiction. While many make a joke of the story others try hard to locate the time and place of the event. It is to their loss that the deep beauty and truth of the message has been missed by those who trivialize it.

To a lesser extent we could say the same about today's Gospel story.

If only the time and energy had been spent on discovering and living the message contained in these lessons, we would have an immensely better and happier world and people alive with hope for the world to come.

Any story in the Bible, whether it is fact or fiction, is there only to lead us to a deeper realization of the truth about God, about our relationship with him and with each other. From this point we can ponder the wisdom and understanding of human nature contained in the readings.

The human race and individuals are created by God with everything we need. Then God gives us more than we are by nature. He gives us grace, the gift of his own Spirit. We are destined to live together in harmony, sharing our gifts, complementing each other from the variety of those gifts among us. We are called to respect each other, God's creation, and thus the creator himself. The very differences between male and female are God's instrument, his continuing plan.

Each one has all that he or she needs to be the person God has called into existence and has destined for eternal life with himself.

The story simply tells us that his plan is disrupted by the sin that disrupts it still. We want more. We want to have more than we need. We want to be more than we are. People take things into their own hands, preferring their way to God's way. Gratification of desire takes precedence over the esteem, comfort, well-being or happiness of someone else.

The greed and selfishness expressed in the words "So she took" continue to wreak destruction on the people from whom the fruits of the earth are unjustly taken.

Self-gratification drives people to take the self-esteem, the good name, the property and even the life of others. Greed has destroyed the balance of nature and continues to do so. It has driven people from their land and made them strangers in their homeland. While we continue to accept such injustices and to justify them by belittling the dispossessed of the world, we continue to reach out and take. While we say nothing and do nothing we let the law of evil take the place of God's law of creative goodness.

Jesus came to call us out of the mess and give us his strength and love. Immediately the same temptation came upon him.

"Turn stones into bread" is the temptation of the quick fix. We can take the easiest way. But we must ask if the easiest way is the way that will take from another. A lie, a bribe, a word to ruin my opponent cannot be justified by the temptation "you need it, you deserve it, it's for the family."

"Jump" is the temptation to be more than we are, to

pretend, to deceive the "fools." Are there people who never know who they really are?

"Worship me." "Forget the rules, morality, justice. Get what you want. It is yours for the taking. Anyone who stands in your way is not a person but an obstacle."

We are all faced with decisions. Only if we live in the spirit of Jesus will the devil depart and angels minister to our world.

Second Sunday of Lent

For Peter, James and John it must have seemed that the kingdom had come. There on the holy mountain Moses and Elijah came to welcome its coming and its king. Here is the place of the new tent of meeting with God. What they had heard just before—that Jesus was to suffer and die—was forgotten in the ecstasy of this glorious moment. Here was the glory, the power, the divine gift. Here we stay. Here is the center of the universe.

But the voice of God called attention again to his living Word: "This is my Son, the Beloved; he enjoys my favor. Listen to him." Yes there was more yet to hear, more yet to learn, more yet to experience. This was not the end, but encouragement to go on, further affirmation of their own discipleship and of the mission of Jesus.

They must stand up, free from fear, and look again at Jesus. All else was gone from sight and hearing. Here was the kingdom, "They raised their eyes and saw no one only Jesus."

Delightful and awe-inspiring as it was to be there, they must come down to earth again and walk the plain with Jesus. The experience was wonderful, but secondary to what was to come. The essential message contained in his death and resurrection is superior to any mystic experience or privileged vision. Indeed, this day's experience will make sense only as remembered and viewed in the context of the glory of the risen Christ. Then they will know the wonder of his reality and what awaits them. They will know that what they have glimpsed here is something of the glory of humanity raised up by the one who says, "This is my Son, the Beloved."

All of this because they accepted the invitation to be alone with Jesus. To be alone with Jesus is not for the fainthearted. It is risky business. Yet it is a component of our growth in faith, hope and love. Jesus calls us to pray together, to gather together and break the bread and drink the cup in commemoration of him. He calls us to bring his forgiveness and love and the gifts of his creation to each other. But we are also invited to be alone with him, to listen to his words and to his call to the mountain and from the mountain to whatever he calls us to do and to be.

The call of Abraham is the story of one listening to God and responding. Like the disciples, he walks out into the unknown. Like the disciples, this is only the beginning of a long and sometimes bewildering journey. Like the disciples, God will see him through.

We disciples need to give God some time and quiet; to be still and know that he is God. He is God, not to be feared; because he is God who says also of us and to us, "This is my beloved."

Third Sunday of Lent

Reading this beautiful piece of literature from St John's Gospel, we sense the contrast between a person in touch with himself, at home with reality and with God, and another totally distracted and out of touch with the things that matter. Then this woman meets Jesus. She actually stops for a while.

At first she talks and remains distracted. She attempts to sidetrack serious thought into a religious argument.

The Samaritan woman is all around us still. In many ways we are like her. It is better to be busy than suffer the pain of reflecting and perhaps changing or hearing a call to undertake an unwelcome task. It is easier to talk about religion than about God or Jesus or prayer or actually to pray.

The messages of the first three Sundays of Lent are many. (The messages of today's readings are many.) They have one thing in common. This is contained in the words "Jesus was led by the Spirit into the wilderness" (1st Sunday); Jesus "led them up a high mountain where they could be alone" (2nd Sunday); "I who am speaking to you . . . am he" (today).

We need time to let him speak to us. Jesus alone in the desert faces the horror of evil, the fact of his own limitations as a human being and then the wonder of a loving God. He knows the way to go. The disciples alone with Jesus experience more deeply who he is, his vision, their limitations and strengths and then God's call to go on.

Today the woman who sits alone with Jesus beside the well

at Sychar for once in her life is able to hear and listen. Just as the self-knowledge of Jesus and his disciples frees them for the journey towards God, so with this woman. The past is there, the present is real. She is who she is. From this reality she can go forward to whom she is to be in the future.

The one who comes to give the living water of his teaching and life is the divine liberator. It is only by truth that we can be set free. In his dialogue with this child of God there is no pretence. It is true she is Samaritan. He is Jew. He has no hesitation in telling her that "Salvation comes from the Jews." He has no time for half-truths such as "all religions are the same." Truth is the key to freedom. Yet he has no time for false assumptions and bigotry. Nation and place of worship mean nothing. The chosen people are those who worship in spirit and in truth. He invites her to look deeper.

Her relationships seem to have been disastrous. Even now she is involved in an illicit relationship. Jesus does not hesitate to speak the truth about this. That he does not condone it is evident from his words. But that he does not condemn her is evident from his loving dialogue and her responses to truth spoken in gentleness and love.

Little did the woman at the well in Sychar realize that she was here and now praying. She spoke to and listened to the Lord. What a change took place.

The disciples were amazed that he was alone with this woman. Like many disciples from that day until this, they have not yet been fully touched by his divine and universal love. Here is a love that is true. She knows that from the gentleness and concern that he shows. It invites a response but leaves her free to make that response.

Fourth Sunday of Lent

God does not see as we see; we look at appearances but the Lord looks at the heart.

Jesus offers us the light to see as God sees. St Paul says to the Ephesians, "You were darkness once, but now you are light in the Lord." When we really live in the Lord with his spirit living in us, the scales fall from our eyes and we see things and people differently.

At the end of today's story the blind man was able to say, "Lord, I believe," and he "worshipped him."

St John tells us of the difficult journey to that point. By today's liturgy the Church calls us to remember all who are making that journey. We remember particularly those praying and searching during their participation in the Rite of Christian Initiation of Adults. At the end of their journey we pray that they too may be able to say with love and understanding, "Lord, I believe" and, with joy, "worship him."

Our call from today's liturgy is to continue that search ourselves. "Believers" still kill each other, destroy the environment for greed, hate or disparage people different from themselves, never share anything important with them whether wealth or effort or forgiveness. Who is the God those "believers" worship? Is there something of those evils still in us? How different is our view from the way God sees things?

As we ponder today's Gospel we realize that everyone in the story was a "believer." The disciples who thought physical disability was the result of the man's or his parents' sins, the neighbors who would not look at the facts, the Pharisees who made God's law of love a trivial rule by which to condemn, the Jews who sought every possible way to escape a love that may cause them to change their minds, the parents who would rather not be involved than to risk their status in the community.

The least of all, as far as status was concerned, was the man born blind. From his need and his poverty he is able to ask for something. He is humble enough to do as Jesus asked. He receives his sight. But that is, in a way, the beginning of further troubles. Remember the chosen people in the desert saying that they would rather have been left as slaves than to face the trouble of being free? This man faces the trouble that his freedom brings him. His stand by the truth is strengthened by the gratitude he feels for the one who has reached out and touched him. He continues the journey. He receives the gift of light and sight that leads to eternal freedom. His journey has only just begun again.

So we are believers. There is no such thing as a static Christian. Called by Jesus and enlightened by his teaching, the Christian is impelled to go deeper and deeper, to ask again and again, "Am I really light in the Lord? Is the one to whom I say, 'Lord, I believe,' really Jesus who is the image of the Father, creator and lover of all?"

"Lord, that I may see."

Fifth Sunday of Lent

In word and in powerful action Jesus states who he is: "I am the resurrection and the life." Belief in him results in eternal life.

In dramatic terms St John describes the climactic miracle in the journey of Jesus to his own death and conquest of death.

"Lord, the man you love is ill." Surely a cry to the love of God on behalf of all humanity. "The ones you created out of love are sick and heading for death." Jesus sees to it that our soul sickness does not lead to death but will end up in God's glory and his glory.

Yet he came in his own good time. At whatever time Jesus came to confront evil and death, he would have to risk the doubt, the ridicule, the stones of those who have a vested interest in the destructive, self-centered forces of evil.

As he entered the confused world of all the people in this story, as he entered the confused world of historical time and place, so he enters the world of every time and place. He comes to bring comfort, understanding and the truth that will free us. He comes to bring life without end. Yet he continues to weep and feel the pain caused by the unbelief, greed and bigotry of those who stand about and mock. In reaching out to human beings Jesus knows the risk but takes it. His faithful followers, like their Lord, go in his steps. Their fate will be the same as his. It is in these that he continues to call out to God, to weep for justice and understanding, to suffer and to die.

Yet there is humanity, like Lazarus locked in a tomb. There are so many stones to be rolled away and so many man-made barriers to truth and freedom and loving communications. "Take the stones away," is the command of Jesus. Yet we hesitate because of whom we will see or touch. We must first risk the smell that will be released when evil is uncovered in our society and in ourselves. But unless we roll the stone away there will be no healing, no life.

To all human beings Jesus cries out in a loud voice, "Here! Come out! Come out of that dark place into the light." Lazarus takes the first hesitant steps into new life. Like all of us, "his feet and hands bound with bands of stuff and a cloth around his face." Then to him and to us "unbind him, let him go free."

Jesus calls us as he called Lazarus to freedom from the inhibitions and fears that hold us back and that cover the beautiful face that God created. It is a freedom that will let us worship him wholeheartedly and release us to love and serve as he does. It is a freedom that will create the unity for which he longed and prayed.

Passion Sunday

In this holiest week we, the Church, are immersed in this magnificent event of our salvation. By this sacramental re-presenting, God seeks to touch us deeply that we might respond in love and gratitude. Then being thus open with his love, our union with God will be deepened. In him we will live and move and have our being.

It is by this openness to God that Jesus brings salvation to the world. In the events made present today and during this week Jesus does and says very little. Our redemption is achieved through his eternal "yes" to the Father, being spoken in flesh and in time.

Jesus speaks the truth and cannot step back from it. There is one God. He is the eternal Son of God. The Holy Spirit is the gift to all without discrimination. God's command is love without exclusion. Loyalty, to the Father and to God's will and message, will bring sorrow to the point of death. People will still want their own way which will inevitably end in injustice and hatred. Rejection of God's way will end in rejection of Jesus. He will be misunderstood, maligned, deserted and hated. From the scourging, condemnation, mocking, the sorrow caused to his mother, his own shocking death, it is impossible to "save himself." For it is impossible for him to please another by denying God. There is only one response possible for total love: "Thy will be done."

Jesus saves here not by word and action but by "passion." He saves by actively accepting the truth and its consequences. The rest is in the hands of the Father.

St Matthew presents us with the Savior, who from his arrest until the end scarcely says a word. Jesus makes three utterances. Each states who he is: "You will see the Son of Man seated at the right hand of the Power and coming on the clouds of heaven." Secondly, the kingdom is present with him and through him. Lastly, "My God, my God, why have you deserted me?" Yes he is one with the power of heaven. He is also one with all who cry out from their earthly suffering and limitation. He is one of us. Jesus uses the prayer of his people. Here he makes his own the words of Psalm 22. Being in deep human distress the Psalm ends: "And those who are dead, their descendants will see him, will proclaim his name from generations still to come, and these will tell you of his saving justice to a people yet unborn; he has fulfilled it."

In this all-important account of his last hours on earth it is not Jesus taking control. Nor is it the evil that takes control. By the power of the spirit of Jesus, God is master of the events. It is ultimately his will that is done, not in suffering, blood and death but in the human spirit overcoming these things. Jesus leaves his destiny to God, yields up his spirit. God will take the action. This is not the end.

Easter Sunday

Jesus called on and exercised God's power over death at the resurrection of Lazarus.

Today's celebration is of a resurrection sublimely different. Lazarus rose to die again. Jesus rises no more to die. The rising of Lazarus was for one man and gave a message of hope to all. The resurrection of Jesus is not only for Jesus, but to give a message of his divine approval to all. It is resurrection for all. As St Paul wrote to the Colossians, "You have died, and now the life you have is hidden with Christ in God. You too will be revealed in all your glory with him."

Through the resurrection human nature enters the divine realm. The natural place of the divine Son is with the Father. He is in heaven. But now forever human nature is one with the divine nature in the one human person Jesus. Human nature enters heaven.

This is the wonder, the joy, the gift of Easter Day. Christ has carried us up to heaven. This is why the waters of baptism figure so largely in the rites of this holy time. It is by our baptism that we are immersed in Christ. We become one body with him. Being one with him we are destined to be where he is. The rightful place of the risen Christ is with God. We are that risen Christ.

It is for this reason that sin is such a tragedy. The Christian, being one body with Christ, is destined to live as Christ lived, to die as Christ, and to rise with him.

Lazarus came from the tomb inhibited by the binding cloths and blinded by the cloth around his face. In today's

Gospel the same John who wrote those things tells us of the risen Lord. Today the risen One has left behind all that binds humanity. The resurrection is of an entirely different order. St John goes to the trouble of telling us of the neat way in which the cloths were left and that they were left. Here was no grave robbery. Here is the gracious act of God who created all that is human, all that humans need, and then asks respect for it. But all that humans need is surpassed by the sublime wonder of the risen life. They are left behind.

For John and Peter the empty tomb is like a key that unlocks those sayings of Jesus and the words of the Scripture shared in their memories. This is what "he must rise from the dead" meant. Too wonderful to comprehend before, now understood. God cares that much.

The longing love of Mary of Magdala had brought her to the tomb, had made her run to the apostles. It still causes her to seek and weep. It would soon be satisfied when she would hear her name "Mary" spoken in love again by the risen Lord. Yet this would be only a shadow of the final joy of her final welcome to where he is. This too is our hope.

Second Sunday of Easter

St John begins his Gospel with a clear statement about the one whose glory we have seen. "In the beginning was the Word, the Word was with God, the Word was God." Now, having let us experience the Word made flesh and see his glory, John ends with the same declaration of truth. From Thomas, who wanted to see and touch before believing, comes the act of faith. Here before him is not only his Lord, but, "My Lord and my God." Then from Jesus an acceptance of Thomas' dramatic conclusion. What Thomas had said is true: "Happy are those who have not seen and yet believe." Generations to come will be blessed with happiness here and in heaven through faith in Jesus their Lord and God.

For the disciples the resurrection is God's seal on Jesus and his teaching. But it is more than this. It is the achievement of our reconciliation with God, the gift of eternal life, the gift of unity with the divine being. It not only brings forth faith from Thomas, but a response of hope, and as Peter puts it, "We have a sure hope and promise of an inheritance that can never be spoilt or soiled and never fade away, because it is being kept for you in heaven." It is a "cause of great joy" even in times of trial.

Thus the first message to the disciples gathered as a body is "Peace be with you." Then "As the Father sent me, so I am sending you." With the spirit of Jesus in their hearts and in their minds and on their lips, they are to proclaim the message of peace through hope. They are to call people together in a spirit of forgiveness. They are to proclaim to their fellow human beings that God forgives whomever asks forgiveness. It is possible for people to forgive and receive forgiveness, God's forgiveness. The acceptance of forgiveness, the forgiveness or retention of sin is up to us.

Is it possible to achieve the unity, peace and love that comes through forgiveness offered and accepted by all?

The Holy Spirit gives the answer to that question in the lives of those freshly filled with his life: "The whole community remains faithful to the teaching of the apostles, to the brotherhood, to the breaking of bread and to the prayers."

Through their faith, hope and love the spirit of God was released and Jesus became present in all those ways mentioned above in the Acts of the Apostles. They were released from rivalry and avarice, from the desire to possess while others were in need and were able to praise God in joy together.

As the joy of God was seen in the face of the risen Christ, it was seen in his body, alive and active there in Jerusalem. In a Church such as this people will recognize and proclaim their Lord and their God.

Third Sunday of Easter

During his life on earth Jesus had no difficulty with people who were ignorant and sinful or wanting in some way, as long as they knew their need. It was when they saw they had need of a savior that they were able to ask for help. His help was ready in coming. He has assured us that if we ask we receive. If we begin from the truth of who we are, knowing our needs, and ask his help, his power will come to completion in our weakness.

But there were those who were really blind, who refused to look any further than where they presumed themselves to be. They made statements from their presumed knowledge but needed to ask no questions except to trick him. They had no needs.

Today's readings have a refreshing frankness about them. Peter calls for attention, then begins by letting people know where they stand. This is where you start from. "This man (Jesus) . . . you took and had crucified by men outside the Law." Some would say, "That is hardly the way to win friends and influence people." Enlightened by the Holy Spirit, Peter knew the sin had to be recognized, admitted and then repented before it could be forgiven. Growth and maturity in any relationship can only take place through truth.

So also in Peter's letter. Before they start they must face the fact that God has no favorites. He is frank about the "useless way of life your ancestors handed down." They need freedom from this. Christ is their freedom.

It is in this Gospel we may recognize ourselves. The two disciples are on more than a journey measured by seven miles. They are not self-satisfied Pharisees who know that Jesus is out of their way. Yet something prevented them from recognizing him. They have a journey to complete.

Here too is the frank but apparently inviting confrontation in truth: "You foolish men! So slow to believe the full message of the prophets . . ." Selective use of the Scriptures, selective acceptance of the teaching and practice of the Christian life will always be that something preventing full recognition of Jesus. It was not enough to accept the passages about a glorious Messiah or a loving, gentle Jesus and leave out the servant of God suffering on behalf of others, standing for truth, the crucified Jesus.

For us as for those disciples the longing is there for unity with God through Jesus. We now can identify with "Did not our hearts burn within us as he talked to us on the road . . ."

It was when they stopped, gave welcome to him, gave him time and broke bread with him, that "their eyes were opened and they recognized him." It was not the physical presence of Jesus that would send them out with changed and deepened faith. When "he had vanished from their sight" his Spirit remained and sustained them for the journey back to Jerusalem and to the eternal city of God.

Fourth Sunday of Easter

The flock of Jesus, the Good Shepherd, is not led into submission and captivity, but to freedom. The leadership of Jesus is a leadership to which we should all aspire. He reveals its purpose: "I have come so that they may have life and have it to the full."

The liberty offered by Jesus, if accepted, will result in his followers reaching their full potential.

In this Easter season we realize more fully that that potential is not only the fully liberated, actualized human being living in harmony with all creation, but it is the risen life with God in Christ.

For this reason Jesus has harsh words for those who steal and kill and destroy. He is not only speaking about killing in the sense of murder. He speaks of those who steal freedom, kill the spirit, murder the child in us.

Jesus is the only gate through which to enter into the real pasture of full life. The wonder of this pasture is that we do not have to go anywhere to find it except to follow him into the reality of our own being. The kingdom is within us and all around us. The journey is one of that sort which follows the way, keeping an eye on the Good Shepherd. We allow his being to be at home in us. We are courageous enough to live in his light and to look. Is what I find the way of the Good Shepherd or the way of "this perverse generation"?

It is on this journey of the truth that St Peter invites those potential followers of Jesus. He begins with the reality, "God has made this Jesus whom you crucified both Lord and Christ." This is where they are and who they are. They begin by accepting the terrible reality that they were wrong and that their error led to this. The search began when they accepted the reality. Then the question could be asked, "What must we do?" Repentance is followed by baptism and the gift of the Holy Spirit.

The Good Shepherd has spoken through Peter, the shepherd of the flock. Jesus has called through the frank truth of Peter. The Good Shepherd is not a pretty plaster statue. He is truth and life. If the truth is hard to face, Jesus gives us the courage to face it. He assures us that we are safe in our own comings and goings in search of the full and rich pasture. We "will go freely in and out and be sure of finding pasture."

Fifth Sunday of Easter

The evil of pride is destructive of any relationship, whether between human beings or with God. It is destructive because it is fed by the lies of presumed self-sufficiency and perceived superiority. Since the proud are unable to admit the need to ask, whether for help, knowledge or understanding, or to be forgiven, isolation and ignorance compound in them.

There is a beautiful simplification in the truth expressed by the lives of the humble. They know or attempt to know their gifts and their limitations and to respond in a positive way to these. They are gifts to us all.

Remember St Thomas' frank humility, that ability and freedom to speak from the truth about himself? "Unless I see . . . I refuse to believe" (2nd Sunday of Easter). Jesus did not reject him because he was lacking in something. Rather if he had pretended, there would have been no more growth. Yet from the truth, blessings and truth issued in abundance for Thomas and for us. Jesus appears again, is seen, touched and declared to be "Lord and God."

In today's Gospel, the frank admission of Thomas that he doesn't know what Jesus is talking about again brings a positive, loving revelation from Jesus. Through the humble accepting of Thomas and his courage to ask the questions we are all blessed with this outpouring of wisdom.

In response to Thomas and to Philip Jesus answers perennial questions . . .

The mystery of God himself can be understood in no better way than by looking at Jesus. "To have seen me is to have seen the Father." What is God like? Look at Jesus. From the baby in the manger, identified with our weakness, to the dying man on the cross, suffering with us, yet forgiving totally, to the risen Lord, accepting back and confirming his wondering followers, Jesus is all love, forgiveness and the compassion that results in saving action.

The mystery of life and the call of its journey are uncovered by Jesus in his reply to Thomas. The way to live is as I have lived. The truth I have revealed in word and living will be your guide to life to the full and to life inexpressably beautiful forever.

"Whoever believes in me will perform the same work as I do myself." The quality of belief that follows through to action and permeates life will produce the life of Jesus in us. As Jesus was the expression of God so will the faithful followers live his life and bring to the world the presence of God in extraordinary ways.

Sixth Sunday of Easter

Last week we reflected on the words of Jesus, "To have seen me is to have seen the Father." For Jesus is the image of God. He is also the father of the new and wonderful life in the disciples. The insights into God's relationship with the world, to the inspiration engendered by his teaching, the freedom that it has brought, the courage it promises, he is the generator of all this in their hearts and wills.

Now in the very atmosphere around them and in the things that Jesus is saying, they feel the threat of his imminent departure.

Are they to be left like orphans who have been cut off from their immediate source of life? Jesus answers their fears.

He too sees the inevitable outcome of his mission of truth. The spirit of worldly ambition and greed can never receive his spirit. The two are incompatible. Selfishness and pride cannot see the point of it all. This spirit of evil will have its way for a while, or so it would seem. But God's love is stronger than the death that evil brings.

Jesus, the incarnation of God's love, will ask the Father to pass on his Spirit so that the disciples will hear the presence of God. It depends only on their response in love. "If you love me you will keep my commandments" then "That Spirit of truth" will be "with you forever."

The physical presence of Jesus is precious to his friends. It is his Spirit, however, that is the abiding gift that brings life and the understanding, wisdom and courage to live his life. It is his Spirit within them that will last and raise them up.

His going from their sight will only heighten their awareness of his presence and power among them. They already possess this Spirit. They need to be made aware of the Spirit, to recognize his presence and to feel his power. The outflowing of understanding awaiting them will empower them to communicate the message and the power to others.

It is no longer a matter of physical power or the power of the law. It is love that brings the presence of God. It is love that motivates the disciples of Jesus to keep his covenant, for love is the basis, their reason for being, even their final end. The revelation of Jesus comes through love and ends in love. "Anyone who loves me will be loved by my Father, and I shall love him and show myself to him."

In the Acts of the Apostles we see the realization of the promise of Jesus and of the fidelity of the disciples whose loving hearts and open minds received the Spirit and dispersed the holy gift with joy.

Seventh Sunday of Easter

The prayer of today's Mass asks God to help us to do two things that the liturgy of the Ascension brought to mind. "Father help us keep in mind (1) that Christ our Savior lives with you in glory and (2) promised to remain with us until the end of time."

Surely it is these two truths that are present to the little group in the upper room. But it is only by continual prayer that their faith will be sustained. They depend too on the strength and faith of each other. Jesus brought them together. It is by their love for one another and their being together in faith, hope and love that he becomes present.

In obedience to the command of Jesus they remain in Jerusalem and "wait there for what the Father had promised" (First reading of Ascension). Jerusalem was not their home and from all that had happened there it is doubtful that they felt at home there. However, this was the parting request of the master. His will could only lead to good. The whole feel of today's scene from the Acts of the Apostles is one of expectancy. They are here only for a short stop. Something will happen to move them on.

Little did they suspect the wonder to come.

From the power of that wonder they would remember so much of what Jesus had said. They would see the import of it. It is only in the power of the Holy Spirit that they recall, preach and write such treasures as John has written.

The beautiful prayer recorded in today's Gospel was prayed

by Jesus at the Last Supper, but it falls into place as the subsequent events unfold. In the light of the Holy Spirit its true meaning is seen and the depth of its beauty plumbed.

It is as if when Jesus prays about himself, he is praying about his followers. Each thought and expression relating to Jesus and the Father leads straight on to "those you have entrusted to him." He cannot exclude from himself those who have become part of him. His journey in the world has finished. Yet through them he journeys on.

The Ascension of the Lord

Artists, both of visual art and of word and sound, talk of "making a statement" with their work.

Here at the beginning of the Acts of the Apostles St Luke makes a statement regarding the risen Lord. As in any works of art it is not only the work on the subject of the picture but the depth of meaning conveyed to the mind and heart by the whole work.

The celebration of Ascension of the Lord is not merely some sort of icing on the cake of the resurrection. It is the statement of a profound and important message.

Where Luke ends his Gospel, his "earlier work," is where he begins the Acts of the Apostles. The last verses of St Luke's Gospel portray today's scene of the Ascension. This Jesus whose words and deeds Luke recorded is the same Jesus who is taken up to heaven, the same Jesus who continues to teach and to save as the Acts of the Apostles will tell, and "the same Jesus will come back in the same way."

Luke dispels any doubt that may be in the minds of Christians about the union of God and human nature in Christ. The union goes beyond his earthly life. Human nature is taken to heaven. Christ does not divest himself of his humanity like some butterfly, leaving behind the caterpillar. Human nature is not some ugly, sinful thing, unwelcome in heaven. Its union with God in the incarnation endures and has been completed.

What was impossible on our own has been achieved in and through Jesus. By his graciousness God invites us to our new rightful place.

The second statement referred to above is that the divine presence is still with us. The disciples need not stand "looking into the sky" for the presence and power of Jesus. He is still with them. They will have the same Spirit as he had, so that they will be his witnesses testifying to the truth he taught. As St Matthew put it, "know that I am with you always; yes to the end of time."

The life that has gone to dwell eternally in heaven is here on earth. It is wherever they, his faithful followers, are. They carry his message, his power to save, his promise and gift of eternal life. As Jesus has trod the way before them, sent by the Father, so now they set out on the same journey.

It is the real Jesus, God and man, who lives eternally. It is the real Jesus who travels with us in his disciples everywhere until the end of time. In each of his disciples Jesus lives, dies and rises to the Father.

Pentecost Sunday

The swirling force of the wind enveloping the apostles, the tongues of fire resting on each of them, the strange language issuing from their lips were perceptible signs of a greater, unseen wonder. These were outer signs of a supernatural event taking place in the depths of their being. The infinite Spirit, in an extraordinary way, made contact with the human spirit. The two were united: "They were all filled with the Holy Spirit." Here is the wonder of Pentecost. This is the lasting wonder. The signs have passed. Time has made them part of history. The reality they signify will last as the apostles, filled with peace, go, as Jesus was sent, on their mission of forgiveness so that all may declare "Jesus is Lord" and be one in the same Spirit. Beyond this even, this gift of unity with God will never end.

Each of us has received the very same Spirit. The signs were different, the Spirit the same. It is by this Spirit praying in us today that we are gathered in our own time and place to confess to the world and to praise God by declaring "Jesus is Lord."

We bring with us "a variety of gifts." What St Paul wrote to the Corinthians, the Spirit says to us today. The Holy Spirit does not come to us to change what God has made, but to do his work though God's gifts in us. As the Spirit of God anoints us with his being, everything that we are is anointed to the service of God. "The particular way in which the Spirit is given to each person is for a good purpose." To say I have nothing to give or let the gifts go to waste from lack of use or lack of appreciation is to inhibit the work of the Holy Spirit.

For the Lord is "working in all sorts of different ways in different people, it is the same God who is working in all of them." Pentecost continues through the disciples of all times and places.

Upon receiving the Holy Spirit the apostles felt an immediate longing and desire to tell the world of the saving work of Jesus. Their first action was to open the doors and to go down from where they were and out to "every nation under heaven" as represented by the people gathered in Jerusalem . . . The Holy Spirit was communicated with such power that "they were amazed and astonished."

"Light immortal, light divine, visit these hearts of thine, and our inmost being fill" (Sequence) so that this desire to communicate you may enliven whatever gifts you have anointed to your service. Thus may all your children proclaim "Jesus is Lord."

Trinity Sunday

From Advent to Pentecost God's revelation has been read and prayed. We have celebrated it in the liturgy, absorbed it from the tradition living in the Body of Christ.

We have, in this, recalled the love of the Father, "a God of tenderness and compassion, slow to anger and rich in kindness and faithfulness." We have celebrated this love as we rejoice in the fact that "God loved the world so much that he gave his only Son."

We have been with that beloved Son of God and learned that he is son by nature in eternity who comes, in time, to be one of us. We have been touched by his love, moved by the tears he cried with us, the blood he shed and the death and resurrection which took our human nature to heaven.

Many times he promised the Holy Spirit who would live in his followers and continue his work. The coming of that Divine Spirit we celebrated last Sunday.

Now, as it were, the Church stands back and reflects on what has happened. God has been revealed as one God who is Father, Son and Holy Spirit. The mystery of God's being has been unfolded as the history of our salvation was unfolded. It is only in knowing who God is that we are able to be touched by his saving grace. "Eternal life is to know you, the only God, and Jesus Christ whom you have sent" (John 17:3).

Thus from the beginning of the Church the unity and trinity of God were believed and proclaimed.

But we know and love a person not by gazing at a picture or even on a face. We know and love only by communication.

We know and grow in knowledge and love when the communication is free enough, truthful enough, frequent enough and deep enough to let spirit touch spirit. So it is with our knowledge and love of God.

For the blessed it is not enough to know about God. There is a longing and desire to know God. The blessed seek him in the Church and its life, sacraments and teachings, in the community, in service to the weak and poor, in a continuing attempt to understand, forgive and love all, and in their respect for all God has made. There in the quiet of their own being they allow God, in whose image they are made, to communicate himself as he wills.

It is this happiness that is the wish of St Paul for us. His prayer is for the happiness that grows from the perfection that is this search for God. In the search for unity and peace with others this peace of God is found.

May we live in this spirit so that "the grace of the Lord Jesus Christ, the love of God and the fellowship of the Holy Spirit" will be with us all.

The Body and Blood of Christ

In Pentecost we celebrated our receiving of the Holy Spirit. God's Spirit was united with the human spirit of the apostles and through them with every Christian. Thus the many gifts God has given to each of us are brought to the service of the Church and the world, not as separate gifts, but in one body—the Body of Christ.

Today we celebrate the gift that signifies the unity of that body and at the same time brings about its unity in every time and place.

As the Church in all places and times offers Christ to the Father for the salvation of the world, the community is drawn together in its supreme act of worship. In any living body there is only one Spirit. So with the Body of Christ, his Church. The breaking and sharing of one bread is the symbol and cause of this unity. "The fact that there is only one loaf means that, though there are many of us, we form a single body because we all have a share in this one loaf."

Never is the Eucharist an act of private devotion. The third Eucharistic Prayer expresses the prayer of Jesus as we ask the Father to "Grant that we, who are nourished by his body and blood, may be filled with his Holy Spirit and become one body, one spirit in Christ."

Living this unity is the test of the manner in which we receive the Body and Blood of Christ.

Our worship in spirit and in truth is not something we can

see. The visible things are important but not as important as those of the Spirit. The Mass is still the offering of the death and resurrection of Christ, the Holy Communion still the reception of his real presence whether it is in the Mass said on the hood of a jeep in the jungle or in the splendor of St Peter's in Rome. The channel created for the flow of Christ's grace to the world and the quality and freedom of that flow depends on the will for peace, love and unity existing in the worshipping community.

For this reason each time we gather we begin by reflecting on the obstacles to this unity in love. We confess them and ask the Savior to break down the obstacles and to heal. Being Christian our prayer for forgiveness implies that we forgive each other.

Then by open hearts and minds the word of God is received and heard with power. By the Offertory we symbolize our participation and freedom to give, we ask God to accept our sacrifice and proceed as one body in one spirit to offer the Savior to God for all. Then with open hearts we are graced by his presence.

It is this bread of life received in this Spirit that gives us eternal life. As the body of Christ is raised from the dead those who are one with him "will live forever."

The Assumption of the Blessed Virgin Mary

Today we contemplate the kingdom through the eyes of the mystic and through the life of the perfect Christian.

The words written in the Apocalypse about the Church are true of Mary because she is the perfectly redeemed one, the perfect member of the kingdom, the perfect person of the kingdom within. What the Church is in its perfect form on earth and its realization in heaven are achieved in Mary. This is our celebration today.

The Church is the assembly of believers, saved by Jesus, attacked by the evil one, but overcoming the attack to the glory of God.

But the believers live in time and place. We live in the human condition in a world of positives and negatives.

As with all believers, Mary was elated by joy and hurt by sorrow because that is human. When one makes so radical a decision to be God's person, this decision requires making and remaking every time it is challenged. The challenges do not come only from the obvious source—the dragon of obvious evil. They come from family, friends, relatives, politics, culture, nationality and even what some would call religion. They come in a subtler form of a call to be loyal. A loyalty that betrays the truth is no loyalty.

How strong in Mary was the call back to the old ways, to be loyal to the traditions, to the religious leaders who now called her son a blasphemer? Remember the relatives who called him mad? Genuine loyalty, true justice, unselfish love will require suffering as they did for this most outstanding Christian woman. "Look after your own," "blood is thicker than water," "charity begins at home," can all be genuine, but can also be calls to "traitorous trueness" and "loyal deceits,"[1] a "loyalty" that destroys someone else.

Mary's genuine faith and loyalty to the call of universal love did bring her suffering, exile, alienation from the "in group," as they did to the apostles. The sword that pierced her soul neither began nor ended at the foot of the cross.

There are elements in the presumptions of every culture, nation, political group and family that require testing against the principles to which Jesus calls us.

Mary's greatness is linked to a blood relationship with the divine one. But her true greatness, the cause of her oneness with the Risen One—the fact we celebrate today—is found in her faith and her trueness to that faith. She conceived first of all in her heart, before ever in her womb. These are St Augustine's words, not mine.

When Mary accepted God's call she accepted the consequences of that call. We are all asked to do this. Actually living it is the coming of the kingdom, the pledge of resurrection.

Mary's Assumption is the consequence of being totally one with the Risen One. Where he is, she is. It was so on earth, so it is in heaven.

---

[1] *The Hound of Heaven*—Francis Thompson

Second Sunday Ordinary Time

What a wealth of revelation, a source of teaching and a fountain of contemplation is the Gospel of St John. The extract for today is still only in the first chapter and already we have been told of the unity and Trinity of God, the Incarnation and Redemption, God's enduring love and our eternal destiny as his children. Our minds have been invited to contemplate the one who is forever divine light and now comes to enlighten everyone who comes into the world. The Lord becomes flesh and dwells among us.

The Lord become flesh is neither separate and aloof nor is he mere human flesh. We see John the Baptist unaware until now that his cousin is the longed-for one. The life of Jesus seems to have been so much one with our ordinary lives that it was not until this chosen moment of revelation that John was aware. Yet it is surely no surprise that the one who grew in wisdom and grace before God and man turned out to be the lamb of God. This is indeed human as John well knows, but more. He is one "who ranks before me because he existed before me." It is quite clear that Jesus did not exist before John in time. John was older by a few months. It is in eternity that the Son of God exists and ranks before all creatures.

Yet even with all that, in this first chapter of St John's Gospel, we see the destiny of Jesus. "Look, there is the lamb of God that takes away the sin of the world." The destruction of evil, reconciliation with God, the unity of mankind, the price of peace and truth and of eternal life need more than human effort. The title "Lamb of God" points to that destiny and indicates the price to be paid. "Lamb of God" points to his destiny as suffering servant of God, destroying evil by taking the place of his sinful brothers and sisters. The spirit of God rests upon and gives testimony and power that we are more than human testimony and human power. In time he will breathe the spirit into all who look and acknowledge him as Lamb of God.

In every Mass, before we are united in Holy Communion with God and with all his faithful people, we are invited to behold the Lamb of God who takes away the sin of the world. The Spirit who spoke through John the Baptist and John the Evangelist and who rested upon Jesus still speaks to us and calls to us to look, ponder, receive, be filled with the wonder of God which is the gift of Jesus. The more we are attentive to this call, the more we will ourselves be identified with the Lamb of God who takes sin away, begs pardon and peace and communes freely and truthfully with his Father and with all creatures.

Third Sunday Ordinary Time

"The people that walked in darkness have seen a great light, on those who live in the land of deep shadow a light has shone."

St Matthew presents Jesus as this shining light as St John has presented him "The word was the true light that enlightens all . . ."

The light that Jesus brings surpasses all that has gone before. It is a light that will show the wonder of God's love and the life to which he calls all as individuals loved by him and as people called to share this love with each other. Jesus is to enlighten us by sharing his life with us in a way that will make the whole of our being brilliant with the eternal life of God.

As John the Baptist, greatest of prophets, willingly fades into the background with courage and fidelity all partial prophesies find their place. Those who see and understand Jesus now see the law and prophets as shadows of the great reality. The sacred writers of the New Book see God's word, as spoken through the Old Book, as always pointing towards the final Word, not just written and spoken but lived. Everything is interpreted through the minds of those enlightened by the final light.

Here Jesus is the real light to the dark world of both Jew and Gentile. Galilee is the place at the crossroads of both worlds geographically. It is the place of insignificant people, border people in every sense. Here is the man of Galilee, the sign of contradiction, offering to raise up the insignificant and to unite the estranged. There is the way, "For the yoke that was weighing on him, the bar across his shoulders, the rod of his oppression, these you will break on the day of Midian."

But this way is God's way, not ours. The wonder of Jesus, his uniqueness, already shows. He speaks of repentance. We must turn around and see that the only way to freedom, peace and happiness both here and eternally is God's way. This Jesus will say, but will also live. Right here and now he is doing that. His cousin and friend, the one to whose greatness Jesus has testified in glowing terms, is taken prisoner. As Jesus preaches, cures the sick, gathers followers, there is never a word about mustering forces to release John. There is never a word of reprisal or revenge. Jesus lives his teaching. If we are to be his followers we are called to trust God. We may not speak words of peace and perform acts of revenge or violence. He calls us into his life in every sense. God will give the grace to those who ask with a heart open to striving, seeking, changing.

Fourth Sunday Ordinary Time

In last week's Gospel passage Jesus is presented as the great light that dawned on "those who dwell in the land and the shadow of death." That part of St Matthew's Gospel is immediately before today's beautiful passage.

The light, freedom and happiness that Jesus brings springs from an unexpected source. The light of the world pierces through the darkness of self-interest, the false insecurity of preservation at all costs of image, prestige or even life. Happiness comes from God.

The light of truth would have us see that our value comes from God. It is in being what we are, without pretence, that happiness consists. It is in encouraging those around us to live that same freedom that we find freedom ourselves.

The poor in spirit live with the conviction that God exists. Perhaps most people believe that, but are not as willing to risk much or let much go just in case. A certain inner peace comes from this deep conviction. It is a peace that exudes gentleness. There are no rivals. No one has to be removed verbally or physically because they may cause me loss. My integrity is more important than anything that another can take from me. Once I begin to have this gentle attitude the earth's my heritage.

We are called to communion with all others. In mourning with others in their sorrows this solidarity is strengthened and becomes the comfort of all. As others suffer injustices true satisfaction will come, not from the security of my own isolation but from the turmoil of being involved. The hurt of my brother and sister is my hurt. Mercy and forgiveness are like love and generosity, they engender those attitudes in those receiving them. They touch the forgiving heart of God and the hearts of human beings.

The pure in heart can do no crooked deed, they act from a pure motive. Their thoughts and words and actions are from the font of goodness that rests in their heart and all ring true. God in their heart they will surely see. Truly sons and daughters of God, they long for his peace and expend themselves to bring it about.

Such a way of life will be misunderstood. The chosen ones that live by these beatitudes will be called all sorts of names and dealt all sorts of blows. The spirit of greed and worldly power has too much to gain from creating competition and rivalry and factions and war. But rejoice if this spirit is against you. Yours is the Spirit of God and the Kingdom of Heaven is yours.

Fifth Sunday Ordinary Time

From nature and from Scripture we know that God has called us to participate in his continuing act of creation. God, in fact, endows every living creature with the continuing power of renewing the face of the earth. He calls human beings into his plan of loving creativity in a special way. We can choose to act in a way that reflects what we are by creation—the image of God. By every creative deed done in love the face of the earth is renewed. The prophet Isaiah invites us into this creative life: "Share your bread with the hungry, and shelter the homeless poor."

In today's Gospel we see God, through Jesus, inviting us into still deeper participation in his life. Just before this Gospel extract, Jesus has told us of the way to live, in what has become known as the "beatitudes." It was last Sunday's Gospel. Now he tells us that by living in that way we will add something to the world. We are called to the dignity of reflecting the light of the world himself. What we do will make a difference to nature and to the quality of life on earth and to the eternal relationship God destines for all people.

There is no thought of parading our good work for praise or power. It is simply by living a life which reflects the wonder of God's love that the wonder of God's goodness inevitably will be seen and God praised.

If those who receive the message do not live the message others will trample it underfoot as something to be discarded as having no relevance to life. Disciples of Jesus, "you are the salt of the earth." You are the taste of God, the element that makes the difference between a tasteless, fickle, temporary life and a life with taste and lasting goodness.

The light that Christ brought to the world, and is to the world, can shine only through Christ. Here, in the Gospel we ponder today, he is inviting his followers of all times to be one with him. As his teaching develops he will give us deeper insights into this unity in one body and this continued life until the end. Here, in the fifth chapter of St Matthew's Gospel, the gift is already offered. The power of his continued presence, and its effectiveness, is shared with his followers. The strength of its impact and its brilliance will be in proportion to the clarity of the images of God reflecting in it.

Sixth Sunday Ordinary Time

The followers of Jesus are to be light to the world. The only way they can do this is by letting Jesus free them and bring to fullness in them the being of God in whose image they are created and re-created.

This does not involve any change to the laws that guide God's people to justice. But it goes beyond the call to obey laws. We are called to be something, not merely to do and avoid specific things. We are called to be the image of God in Christ. God's beauty, love and goodness have nothing to do with law. He is neither limited in his action, nor called to action by any law. It is his being, that he is, by which and from which he acts. God's existence of beauty, love and goodness is totally nondependent.

Jesus invites his followers to consider the reality of our being. We exist for this free goodness of God. We too are created for beauty, love and goodness.

When we accept that this is so for us, it follows that this is so for all. The people that know this in a depth of knowledge that comes from God need no laws. They could never deliberately destroy one another.

So Jesus takes three examples of destructive, sinful acts to show his followers that creative life lived in God is more than obeying the letter of the law.

It is ultimately destructive of other human beings to kill. But we can choose to destroy others in many other ways.

Hatred, the choice to reject and destroy another, can never be part of the Godlike one.

Lust is a destructive act because another human being is used as a commodity, as an object of self-gratification. Victims of any type of sexual abuse or deception are sadly aware of this. This too begins within. It has nothing to do with mere passing thoughts. It comes from the mind of one whose real desires are converted into plans and whose plans are either carried out or thwarted by something or someone else. The image of the all-loving God needs no law against such things.

The destruction caused by deceitfulness is caused irrespective of conforming to written laws. Once again the person who is the image of absolute truth can be trusted whether words are spoken or written, taken under oath or simply "yes" or "no."

All actions proceed from inside a person. If the person is indeed a temple of God's spirit, law will not become wrong or be rejected or changed, but become superfluous.

Seventh Sunday Ordinary Time

Over the past couple of weeks we have considered the call of Jesus to his followers. It has been a call to reflect what they are by living what they are called to be—the image of God, the continuing presence of Christ: the light of the world.

Today Jesus calls us to that challenging way of life by words as direct as "be perfect just as your heavenly Father is perfect." We may be tempted to say, "That is impossible." Well, say it. It is impossible. But it is not simply by our own power we are called to live this way. It is by the gift of God's love within us. What is impossible by mere human effort is possible by God. This is the first consideration: we call on the Spirit of God.

The second is, of course, that we are not called to the same perfection as God. There can be only one Absolute. Jesus is reminding us of our likeness to God. God is total perfection in being God. Just as he is perfect we are called to be perfect by being what we are—fully human and fully Christian. God's perfection cannot be added to or subtracted from; our perfection consists of continually adding and subtracting, in being one with the continual growth and change that is part of human life.

We see in this talk of Jesus he is calling his followers to change. If they think that virtue consists of being a nice person with those we like and getting even with enemies, they should think again. They should stop, consider God in whose image they are made, see how he acts and apply the consequences of this consideration to their lives.

Jesus puts a few questions to nice people who look after their own and asks, "Are you doing anything exceptional?" So then, he is calling us, his followers, to be exceptional. The Christian life is not just going along with what happens to be socially acceptable or part of the local custom or the common pattern of behavior. Christians are asked to judge their behavior by higher standards and to act accordingly. This needs wisdom, courage and love beyond instinctive love. We need the grace of God to love with his universal love.

We know very well that racism, revenge, spiteful competition, preference of family and friends, exclusion of enemies and those classed as outsiders, enduring unforgiveness are common in any society. Talk that expresses and emphasizes these attitudes is common among nice people. The Christian is called to break the barriers created by these sinful attitudes. We are called upon to be courageous enough to be exceptions.

Eighth Sunday Ordinary Time

The life of an undercover agent or a spy must be a tense existence. While being loyal to one set of values the spy is pretending to be loyal to the powers that oppose those values. Such constant pretence must take its toll. Yet such a person has no conflict of real loyalty. As far as loyalty is concerned conscience is clear.

It is quite different for one who leads a double life by serving whomever or whatever serves his or her own selfish ends. It is this miserable existence that Jesus condemns. "No one can be loyal to two masters." Then he makes it clear who the opposing masters are. "You cannot be the slave of both God and money."

Do we really accept this Christian teaching? It is not the invention of some theological school or the invention of some latter-day radical. This is Jesus speaking. He puts God and money in two opposing camps.

Money has come into existence to serve us. It saves us carrying about and tallying up the goods and services we exchange as we go about our lives. The follower of Jesus is forbidden to use it as a weapon of power or as a means of gaining preference over others. One who uses money in this way will gradually be persuaded that money is power and power is precious. The end result is the temptation to accumulate money. For such a one, God and God's gifts of nature and grace are too great a risk. They may not work in his or her favor. Money and its power will.

With this as background we can see the importance of the words "surely life means more than food, the body more than clothing." The gathering up of much more than is necessary, taking every precaution in case something goes wrong, covering every contingency: surely these attitudes give no evidence of people who believe and trust in God who tells them through Jesus how precious they are.

It may be hard to convince people to trust God. But we cannot live with two loyalties. Perhaps the reason that some people get no joy from their Christian faith is that they are, in fact, serving two masters. Called to the joy and freedom of Christianity, they see it merely as a set of laws. They will do the minimum required but still be careful in case it lets them down. To obey God is a burden. They have never taken his invitation to enjoy the fullness of life he offers. It is too risky.

There are those who blame their obsession with money on their children. We never had these things, we will make sure our children do not miss out. Yet while their attention is turned to accumulation of security, the children are deprived of the things of the spirit. Haven't so many of us experienced this and listened to the sorry story of so-called spoiled children turning on their parents who have "given them everything."

Jesus knows what he is talking about. Life is more than what we eat or put on or the things we store up. If we live in union with God and we love each other day by day, the future will be all right.

Ninth Sunday Ordinary Time

Here Jesus makes no distinction between "the will of the Father in heaven" and "these words of mine." He calls people to listen to and obey his words which are the expression of the will of God.

What, then, are "these words of mine," this "will of my Father in heaven"? Remember what has gone before this extract of Matthew's Gospel? We have been reading it over the last few Sundays. It is known as the Sermon on the Mount. Now this command of Jesus to his disciples comes at the end of that discourse. He finishes his instruction on the way to live with these words. He tells us that our actions of loyalty to his teaching must coincide with our own words and expressions of worship and loyalty.

Jesus calls us to listen to his words in such a reflective way that they will be always and everywhere the guide and standard of our actions. We are to listen in prayer so that our desires are simply what God wants. Our will and God's will coincide. To live in such a way needs the deep rock foundation that Jesus speaks of here. Even when we are conscious of acting or speaking in a way that is contrary to the teaching of Jesus, we let this mistake or sin or lapse be another point of learning. We need to know and realize and love God's presence within us more deeply still. The standard that becomes part of life will gradually be, "Is this what Jesus would have done or said?"

To see the way of life that Jesus calls us to, we look back over these last few Sundays and read the Sermon on the Mount. It is a call to live in human terms the universal love, total forgiveness, unselfish generosity and deep compassion of God as expressed not only in the words but in the life and actions of Jesus. It is a call to compare the ways of getting on in the world with the way of Jesus. His way is total trust in God. The other spirit will offer quick solutions to our problems. It is expressed by violence, lies, overbearing outbursts, bribery of some sort, cheating or revenge. Or we may even choose merely not to be involved, to remain safe wherever we are and close our ears and shut our eyes. It is then that the compassionate Jesus calls us to reflect his spirit of love and says, "It is not those who say to me 'Lord, Lord' who will enter the kingdom of heaven, but the person who does the will of my Father in heaven."

Tenth Sunday Ordinary Time

"It is not the healthy who need the doctor, but the sick." It is refreshing to realize that the sick, the tax collectors and sinners whom St Matthew is writing about here are himself and his friends. One of the intriguing things about the Gospels' authors is their matter-of-fact way of writing about the apostles. There is no cover-up, no creation of heroes of majestic stature. St Matthew, tax collector and sinner, is called by Jesus. Like the fishermen, he leaves the past and its trappings and goes forward. He follows Jesus. It is beautiful to see that he does not believe he is too good now for his former friends, or too bad for Jesus. Matthew leaves his comfortable house, he leaves his job and its location and goes to Jesus. But like the other disciples he introduces Jesus to others. He is proud to be the follower of Jesus and not ashamed to be who he is or ashamed of his friends. He has a long way to go but he has moved. The same man gradually grows to something greater. Jesus is happy to be with the friends of Matthew. He is there not judging but as one who loves them. Therefore there is no need for pretence. He does not deny that they are sinners or tax collectors. Matthew, unlike the Pharisees, has the advantage of knowing his need. It is from this knowledge of need that the divine doctor can heal.

Divine truth can get nowhere while human pretence persists.

The mercy that St Matthew writes about in this account of his call by Jesus, the mercy that Jesus requires before sacrifice, is mercy that Matthew required himself, accepted and received.

The followers of Jesus will offer his sacrifice in the enduring sacrament that he will leave in his testament spoken at the Last Supper and achieved in the Paschal Mystery. But it is the sacrifice of Jesus. It is impossible for us to receive the fruits of that sacrifice in the way Jesus wants unless we offer it in unison with him and his Spirit. We are called to worship in Spirit and in truth. What we pray and offer and receive is the God of mercy—Jesus the Redeemer. It is obvious that mercy in our own hearts is a prerequisite to do this. We offer in his name.

At the beginning of our liturgy we ask forgiveness, but we are also to say just before receiving the Lord—"forgive us as we forgive others."

If we live the words of our act of sacrifice, we must accept forgiveness and mercy and give forgiveness and mercy. Like Matthew we need the saving love of Jesus. Like Matthew we faithfully accept these. Like Matthew we accept, love and forgive others.

Eleventh Sunday Ordinary Time

The shepherds of Israel had betrayed their trust, they had been warned many times by the prophets, as Ezekiel has warned them, "Shepherds, the Lord says this, Disaster is in store for the shepherds of Israel who feed themselves! Are not the shepherds meant to feed the flock . . . my flock has been scattered . . . no one bothers about them and no one looks for them." The promise of God: "I myself shall take care of my flock and look after it" (See Ez. 34:1–11).

Here today we see the Good Shepherd full of compassion for people who have neglected caring for each other, whose religious leaders have cared for themselves and made religion a job. Jesus sees the goodness hidden in the rich and generous hearts of people. He confides his concern to his disciples and asks them to be one with him in prayer to the Lord of harvest. It is laborers that Jesus longs for, not just official representatives of some organization. Pray for laborers!

But there are other things for us to remember as we all labor in our own way in the Lord's work.

Pray from concern, he asks them.

It is Jesus who gives the authority. The Lord is the shepherd of his people. This does not change. Whatever power of word or healing or authority over evil they have, it is God's power, they are merely ministers of his power: "He gave them authority."

It is significant that the twelve apostles are named here.

Jesus has not gone to the rich, the powerful, those who already have competence of their own. He has not called on the learned or the clever who will use their own knowledge and methods. The twelve, as far as we know them up to this point in the Gospel, are probably not the twelve we would have chosen.

But that is just the point. Jesus is the shepherd. He has the knowledge and the power and the wisdom, and in the end the grace that they will pass on. They will learn that the lowest among them is the greatest precisely because of this ability to pass on the gifts without adding or detracting from this pure light. For this little disciple it is nothing of self, nothing for self.

They are to look for the lost sheep of the House of Israel—the neglected chosen ones. Just as Jesus has not gone to the self-sufficient, so with them. The sick, lepers, possessed, even dead. There is not much social climbing there. There is only need. You would think it wasn't very necessary to ask them not to charge people like lepers who were not even worthy of any contact in the society. But St Matthew drives home the point, "Shepherds feed the flock—not yourselves. Remember you are only handing on God's gifts and these are free."

Immediately after, Jesus tells them that they have no need to store up anything for the laborer deserves his keep. They will be provided for.

Twelfth Sunday Ordinary Time

It seems, from those who tell their stories, that the great acts of heroes are sometimes done on the spur of the moment. These almost always spontaneously react to the drastic need of others. At other times brave people, although frightened, take the risk for the love or concern for another. It seems that in the second case actual bravery is more evident and more inspiring.

Jesus cannot forbid his followers to be frightened for fear is a human instinct and human nature is God's creation. What he is asking of his disciples is that although they may be frightened, fear is not to overcome their commitment to him. The only thing to fear is betraying the trust, acting falsely, acting contrary to our belief in order to save ourselves in some way.

Eventually all material things will be lost. The loss of anything, even life, cannot be compared with this loss of the eternal gift we all possess. Everything we have except this can be taken by force. People have suffered the loss of possessions, freedom of movement and association with others, health, mental stability, life itself at the hands of others. No one can capture conscience. No one can take possession of my mind. Only I can decide in the things that really matter.

Jesus himself has spoken openly the truth he must communicate for our salvation. He will suffer for it later but God's will must be done. He himself will have to reflect on the abiding care that the loving Father has for all his creatures.

He will be frightened but he will know in the depths of his being that there is no need to be afraid. He will fall into the ground but will be lifted up as something infinitely more precious than hundreds of sparrows.

Now is the time for him to speak of the wonders of the kingdom in the quiet and accepting atmosphere in the community of the disciples. Their time will come to speak out and face the consequences. The consequences, in fact, were being experienced even as St Matthew recorded these sayings and events in the life of Jesus.

There are times and places of overt persecution. There are times and places when the temptation to betray by silence is less obvious. Attitudes, words and deeds contrary to the kingdom exist in every society. Sometimes the evil becomes part of the system as in Nazism or atheistic Communism. Sometimes it infiltrates into a society under the name of freedom and democracy. Any attitude, word or deed, that lessens the dignity of a fellow human being or group of people is contrary to the kingdom. Racism, greed, religious discrimination, violence, sexual attitudes, words and deeds that indicate that a person is merely a source of pleasure or a thing to be used, profiteering from things that degrade human beings, can all be approved by people who say "Lord, Lord."

There are obvious times and places to speak up and take a stand. At such times and places silence hardly proclaims the kingdom from the housetops. Cold-blooded heroism is real heroism. Among so-called friends it is more heroic still.

Thirteenth Sunday Ordinary Time

"Anyone who does not take his cross and follow in my footsteps is not worthy of me." What is this cross we are to take? It is the journey we are to take in following in his footsteps. For the cross is the redeeming act of Christ and all his footsteps led to this.

By initiation into the life of Christ we are initiated into his way of living, his way of dying and his resurrection. Being true to Christ will cost us something. If it does not we should stop and look at the way we are living. This cost is what Jesus means by the cross. Fidelity to his way of living is the step-by-step path in his footsteps.

We would all hope that there would be no reason for us to choose between Jesus and father and mother, son or daughter or anyone else dear to us. We would hope that faithfulness to them would be the same as faithfulness to Jesus. If, however, loyalty to a person, a party or country is at odds with conscience informed by Christ's teaching, then the truth of that teaching is the only choice for the Christian.

In the time of St Matthew there must have been many who were called from what family and country held dear to go forward in a deepening of all that, in Christianity. But what is true of those times is true of all times. It is never easy for the Christian to keep choosing the way of Jesus in a world which encourages self-interest, family interest, national interest at the expense of others. Principle before profit will call for decisions based on faith.

We are asked to make this faith and those who inspire it a welcome part of our lives and in fact the center of our lives. We welcome Jesus by welcoming and encouraging each other as we strive towards the truth of his call. How we need the cup of refreshment as we travel the journey of honesty, truth and open-mindedness, constant worship of God in truth. As we refresh each other by the encouragement and hospitality Jesus refreshes us. There are those who call the virtuous and the prophet fools when they have suffered some loss through truth. Perhaps we have been called fools ourselves for doing what is right and just. This is the time for encouragement to goodness. "Anyone who welcomes a prophet because he is a prophet will have a prophet's reward."

A prophet's reward was mostly suffering, rejection and death. But the prophet's reward is also the joy of integrity—and eternal life.

Fourteenth Sunday Ordinary Time

Jesus is God, one with the Father in eternal knowledge and love. No one has this total, intimate, absolute knowledge of the Father, who knows the Son in everlasting love.

It is an inkling of this love and knowledge that Jesus is able to reveal to his chosen. The choice excludes no one except those too clever to listen and that is their choice, not his.

It is the open minds of unprejudiced children, ready to listen and learn, to whom the revelation is made. And those who know everything, have everything in control and can pay to get their way have no need for revelation. People who say "what I believe is what I see and hear" lack the gift of the searching, seeking child who listens in joyful wonder.

Yet what we see and touch is not everything. The everything of Jesus is more than this. The Spirit which directs what we see and touch and know is the essential that makes the difference between misery and happiness. The intangible qualities of love, dedication, faith and hope make the difference between mere animal life and truly and fully human life. It is these things that make us Godlike. It is love that will endure eternally.

In the ecstasy of this love for the Father the prayer breaks from the lips of Jesus, "I bless your Father, Lord of heaven and of earth." Just before this we see that Jesus has not been welcome in the towns of Galilee. Even this disappointment leads him into deeper contact with the Father and from there to bless and thank the Father for these little ones, mere children who have stayed faithful and hang upon his words. His beloved fishermen, tax collector and the rest. These people with nothing, possessing everything—the everlasting that has been entrusted to Jesus by the Father—minds and hearts emptied of self-love and self-satisfaction, ready to be filled with everything that really matters.

They carry the burden of weakness and sin and the desire to seek and find and share the knowledge and love they have found. The yoke of Jesus is their yoke, his burden, their burden. It will let them come to be refreshed from the source of his refreshment and strength, let them be in touch with the heart of the eternal and absolute love. Only in this way will the burden of their mission become easy and even joyful and light.

The invitation to come and be in touch and to draw refreshment and strength goes out to all his followers until the end.

Fifteenth Sunday Ordinary Time

It is not surprising that Jesus often uses nature and its functions to describe the kingdom. We are part of nature and the kingdom is a gift planted in our earthly being. If the kingdom is to bear any fruit in us or for others through us it must receive a warm and caring reception from us. The kingdom is not merely a club to which we belong. It, with its living message, needs to be received into our lives and pondered and nourished by prayer and Christ-like action. It needs encouragement and interaction in the community of believers who worship God in one body and in one Spirit.

These things are to the kingdom within and to the Church as a whole as rich, plowed, watered soil is to a seed.

The kingdom and a superficial belonging cannot coexist. That strange thing that Jesus said may seem unfair: "For anyone who has will be given more, and he will have more than enough; but for anyone who has not, even what he has will be taken away." This again is a reflection of nature and of human life. Gifted people who use their gifts with wonder and generosity grow in ways and in relationships they never dreamed of. Gifted people, too self-centered to appreciate what they have, thinking that others have more and driven by envy and self-pity, lose what they have. They have never responded in wisdom and gratitude to what they have. In the parables of the talents Jesus speaks of such as these. But we are all gifted by nature in many ways. So too we are gifted by

God's invitation to the life of grace—the invitation to the kingdom. Jesus speaks of the sad situation of those who will lose everything because they see no value in this pearl of great price.

The seed of God's word is given. They have something. It is not appreciated and received. God's love and life are not given a home. What they have is lost.

He speaks in parables. Those who received the gift are thus given the chance to turn it over in their minds and nourish the message with further contact with Jesus. Those who are content to be where they are, undisturbed, have the opportunity merely to walk away unenlightened. Even what they have is lost.

Jesus continues to offer this choice. Treasure the word deep in the rich soil of our being, nourish it with contact with him, let it bear the fruit that expresses his love to all.

Sixteenth Sunday Ordinary Time

The few verses from the Book of Wisdom and the Psalm make a perfect setting to display the beauty of this parable from St Matthew's Gospel. The liturgy invites us to hear the parable with these words still in our minds and hearts: "There is no God, other than you, who cares for everything," and "But you, God of mercy and compassion, slow to anger, O Lord, abounding in love and truth."

The kingdom of heaven is a result of God's creative beauty: "The sower of the good seed is the Son of Man . . . The good seed is the subjects of the kingdom."

God does something beautiful and creative—and someone makes a mess of it.

What should we do to clean it up?

Jesus gives a gentle message to those who have the purge mentality. Even James and John wanted a quick and deadly purge on the Samaritans who refused to welcome Jesus. "Lord, would you not have us call down fire from heaven to destroy them? He turned towards them only to reprimand them" (Luke 9:54).

This is the same story today: "Do you want us to go and weed it out?"

The bad instinctive answer is so often, unfortunately, the purge. Get rid of the troublemaker, the nuisance, the dissenter.

This mentality gives rise to the persecution by the Church from earliest times until the present. It has taken place in the name of religion, in the name of the Spirit, the State, in the name of the good of all people, by empire builders, Communists, Fascists.

Nazis, even Christians—we ourselves have taken the purge as the solution to our problems.

It is not the mind and Spirit of our God, who cares for everything.

Do these thoughts of Jesus have any meaning in our civilized, democratic, Christian country?

How long is it since you heard "Castrate the rapist, lash the armed robber, hang the murderer"; or perhaps "If they don't want to agree let them go to another Church," or "Do they have to keep changing things?" or "If they want everything as it was 50 years ago we are better off without them."

Doing nothing is not the answer to our problem. Likewise the brutal purge has never achieved anything for the human race. It will never bring us closer to God as a people or as individuals.

Both as individuals and as a Church, Jesus calls on us to go on patiently, seeking his will and doing it.

We have to make practical decisions for ourselves and for the safety and welfare of the community.

Jesus gives us a goal: that which is life-giving, that which makes for true freedom and is creative—in other words those things that are of the kingdom of God.

We pray, we decide, we co-operate with each other and with his grace. We must make decisions and this requires judgment. But he relieves us of the awesome duty of judging the worth of another human being and condemning. He is the judge. We can safely leave God's work to God.

Seventeenth Sunday Ordinary Time

Last week we contemplated the good seed growing in a rough, unweeded field. "The good seed is the subjects of the kingdom." The People of God wait upon their God.

Today Jesus presents the kingdom as a treasure within. We are invited to go on the exciting treasure hunt for holiness. This invitation is to all. Holiness is for all. If we are people of the kingdom, then we are people who prefer nothing else to the kingdom. The kingdom of heaven is like . . .

What is this holiness?

The Church presents the pearl of great price in the setting of the Solomon story. God invites Solomon to ask for anything. Solomon's reply is "give your servant the heart to understand to discern between good and evil." He discarded everything else to seek the pearl of great price—"What does God want? What is my personal response to God so that my life will mean 'Thy kingdom come'?"

How do I get the "taste" for what is best?

Perhaps we may be thinking, "It is easy to know good from evil." If it is as simple as that why do warring peoples of different sides call on God to see them through in their "just" cause? Have you never been involved in a personal dispute, a domestic argument or an attempt to arbitrate two opposite sides who both fight for their "rights"? What of our own decisions in life, our choices between two ways, both presented as good?

The disciple who finds the treasure first of all decides that it is worth more than anything that opposes it. The disciple takes God seriously.

Our first movement towards responding to God's call, then, will be a desire for unity with God, here and forever. The way will often be unsure and even undecided for a long time. We don't stop searching. This desire will need constant nurturing by prayer, the sacraments and a positive response to the good when it becomes clear.

If we are to make positive, creative, life-giving decisions, we must attempt to let God rid us of all prejudice. We want what God wants. Prejudice can cloud the issue. The right decision may or may not favor my bank balance, my prestige, my friends, my ethnic group, the people I get on with. My decision-making, my search for the truth, can all be influenced by the things that the merchant has left behind to own the pearl.

The call for the search is to all. All can possess the treasure of God's spirit. The stories chosen by Jesus tell us that the merchant finds it in his trading, the farmer in the field, the fishermen in their nets, the householder brings out of his storeroom things both new and old. The search begins from where we are. But it is a search.

Eighteenth Sunday Ordinary Time

Last Sunday St Matthew presented us with the person who "goes off happy, sells everything he owns and buys the field" of treasure.

Today we have an example of people who were so rapt in Jesus that they did leave everything to follow him. This may have been only for a short time, but it tells us of the risk of the journey, of the faith required and of the resources that the Lord provides from his treasure house.

Remember how Moses asked the people to follow God's call out of Egypt into the unseen? They followed with enthusiasm. They ended up in the desert. They felt deserted, let down and betrayed. They complained and hankered after the comforts they had left behind. Then Moses pleaded for them and God revealed his presence, giving them food and drink and shelter for the journey.

In this story of God in the wilderness the Moses figure of Matthew, Jesus, the presence of God beyond all those before him, tells us that his God, their God, our God always travels with them. We are invited to look beyond the miracle of providing food to what the call to follow Jesus implies.

The story is about the kingdom, as the parables are about the kingdom.

It reflects the risk we take in saying yes to God and no to safer, surer, more visible gods. It is about the seed that sprang to life on the rock but did not last, and the seed that fell into deep, rich soil. The going is not easy in the wilderness. But the disciple whose life goes down to the rich soil lives in faith through the dry until in God's good time the disciple is refreshed, enlightened and enlivened.

Today's story is life in miniature. The disciples follow with enthusiasm, feel the heat of the journey, feel sorry they ever started. Then there is the real decision: either, "I have had enough, go on without me"; or "I feel let down, empty, but perhaps there is another disciple with a few loaves and a couple of fish. I will ask for help." Gradually the presence of God shines from and through the two little ones—the one in need who has the humility to ask in faith and the one who thinks he has nothing to give, but responds in faith. A miracle takes place. The miracle of God's presence and all-powerful love.

Jesus again is recognized on the journey in the breaking of the bread of human life.

Nineteenth Sunday Ordinary Time

Again St Matthew uses an extraordinary event in the life of the disciples to tell us of the kingdom. Jesus is in the security of the mountain prayer with the Father. They are in the dark, battling a heavy sea with a wild wind against them. He has put them there. ("Jesus made the disciples get into the boat.") Here is the kingdom, the faithful few, all forces gathered to destroy them and the presence of God nowhere to be seen, felt or heard.

Just as those with deep faith were able to come through the desert dryness of last week, so they will see through the turmoil of the storm. They look through the mist and the misty figure is "Truly the Son of God."

How keenly the disciples needed to be reminded of this in the years immediately after the Ascension. Jesus is with the Father while they are sent out to be named blasphemer by their own people and subversive or fool by the Gentiles. Blasphemers and subversives are killed and fools ignored.

But what Jesus says and does is for all times, until the end of time. It is for us, the disciples now. We are told by Jesus to get into the boat and go ahead to the other side.

He assures us that he is close. Whatever the deep darkness, the force of wind against us, the turmoil of the threatening sea, the faithful one comes from darkness to the misty figures, to the realization "Courage! It is I! Do not be afraid. Come." Even when the step is taken uncertainty still causes us to falter.

But the love does not cease and the further call continues to lift us up.

Another beautiful thing in all of this is that we, being one with Christ, are both the people in the boat and the Lord who gives strength to continue the journey.

We are both the needy and the one who gives, the weak and the strong, the mourner and the comforter. There are not, in God's kingdom on earth, those who have all the gifts and those to whom the gifts are dispersed. We are, even at the same time, both the receiver and the giver.

How often is it, that in and after turmoil, the destruction, the loss, the most beautiful elements of human nature rise to call the distressed to hope.

The Lord was not in the mighty wind, so strong it tore the mountain and shattered the rocks, or the earthquake or fire. After the fire there came the sound of a gentle breeze. "And when Elijah heard this he covered his face with his cloak and went out and stood at the entrance of the cave." Through every circumstance in life we are ever called to deeper faith, firmer hopes, truer love. It is a call across the water. It is a call to come out of the safety of the cave.

Twentieth Sunday Ordinary Time

More than once I have got into trouble or been seen to be foolish for being too generous in my response to requests from people who call at the presbytery seeking money. They ask for their fare to the country, money for the next meal, or sometimes have a bargain for sale. I find it hard to refuse.

This is not a statement of self-praise but a cause for self-examination.

Obviously, it is not always helpful to comply with any request without question just to prevent feeling bad for refusing. It can be more helpful to have the courage to refuse, but the care to seek to help the real needs. This is obvious in our relationships with children. But isn't it true that most of us have areas in which we have not grown up. We can still make a fuss when we don't get what we want.

In today's Gospel the disciples ask Jesus to "give her what she wants, because she is shouting after us." The woman is presented to Jesus by his friends as a problem to be removed rather than a human being to be heard, responded to and cared for.

Jesus on the other hand brings things back to the center. How is she in relation to reality and to the great reality, God? What is her life's response to the ultimate? He is sent to bring back "the lost sheep of the House of Israel." Where is she in this great plan of salvation?

The problems of life will go on. Today it is "my daughter

is tormented by a devil." When that goes away it will be something else. Troubles from within and from outside will come and go, just as joys and good fortune will. What makes for happiness and finally eternal happiness through all of this is that pearl of wisdom, that deeply rooted faith, that gift of the presence of God—the kingdom within.

Just as Jesus had led his disciples to deeper faith by the desert and the storm at sea, so he leads this little one to the faith by apparent absence from her concern. As it happened with the loaves and the fish, so the very circumstance of life in which the woman finds herself leads to the Lord. She comes in complete humility, in complete truth of life. She is a woman, a Caananite, her daughter is in a mess, she has her own limitations and her own gifts, her own personality. She comes to the Lord in urgency, without pretence, out of love and deep concern. Her apparent absence from his concern, even to the point of what looks to us like an insult, comes to be like his apparent absence from the disciples in the sea-tossed boat. Again the darkness is prelude to the dawn.

What joy Jesus seems to express when she recognizes the universal love that she has discovered and tapped. Love has broken down the barriers of prejudice that their separate cultures, history and lives have created. More is given than was originally asked.

Jesus does nor merely hand out what we want to keep us quiet or to satisfy his public image. There are deeper, richer treasures in store for those who see beyond the present perceived need and wait upon the pleasure of their Lord.

Twenty-first Sunday Ordinary Time

In many of the great artworks depicting St Peter the artists place the keys in the saint's hands. But often in the background is that wretched rooster—the reminder of St Peter's denial of his friendship with Jesus. The divine is at work in this man but the human remains with all its strengths and weaknesses. It is a summary of the Church itself as well as of its first leader and those who follow him.

The faith of Peter is a divine gift. "It was not flesh and blood that revealed this to you but my Father in heaven." That it is a gift is not an exception. Faith that leads ultimately to heaven has to be a gift to anyone who possesses it. God's own life within us, grace, the gift of the Holy Spirit, heaven are above nature. This has to be pure, free gift from God. Human nature is capable of human life but not divine life. How blessed we are to be honored thus by God with the joy of his infinite life.

The Gospel passage is a wonderful revelation in regard to God's relationship with us through Jesus. The human response to the divine invitation is seen through the man here named Peter—the rock foundation of God's assembled people—the Church.

Jesus draws Peter and the others to this moment of grace and revelation. They have already been captivated by the beauty of his teaching and the integrity of his life. It is revealing to realize that Jesus has not said to them, "I am the

Christ, the Son of the living God." He has asked them, to follow him in the truth. He has asked them to pray, to trust, to seek. Now he asks them what they have heard from others who perhaps do not know him as intimately. Then, what is in your own hearts and minds—share your thoughts. What have you found?

It is all so human; through taking life's search seriously they have come to the point where they are open to God's revelation. Peter's big heart and open mind receive the flood of light. It is through human beings that God has been revealed. Thus it is with the Christ, the Son of the Living God, the revelation of the Father. So it will be through the human beings who will be the foundation of his continuing presence on earth and his continuing revelation. The bond created here will endure. Jesus commits himself to a bond between earth and heaven that will never be broken.

The underworld, death, will be overcome in two ways. It will not wipe out his followers and it will itself be wiped out by their resurrection. His kingdom of light and life will prevail.

However, Peter and the faithful still remain human. The keys of heaven are in his possession but the rooster's piercing crow ever reminds us that it is through limited human resources that God has chosen to forgive, ennoble and inspire. Thus he tells them not to tell anyone—do not reveal half the message. There is more to come. He does not want fanatical followers of "their" Messiah but followers who have the Spirit that will come when all is consummated. We will see a hint of this next week.

Twenty-second Sunday Ordinary Time

Today's Gospel reading follows immediately after last Sunday's. Last Sunday Jesus gave Simon a name full of meaning—Peter, the rock foundation of his Church. Today he calls him Satan. What is going on?

Do you remember that last Sunday's Gospel finished with the words "Then he gave the disciples strict orders not to tell anyone that he was the Christ"? We reflected that he did not want an incomplete message going out about the Messiah. He did not want fanatics taking up the sword to defend his cause.

Today we see that one of the very ones to whom he has entrusted the message, to whom the Father has given the revelation, is the first to take a step in the wrong direction. This same apostle will later on draw the sword in defense of Jesus and cut off a man's ear. Will we never understand that force, brutality, war all cut off listening? They are never the instruments that lead to hearing and understanding God.

When Jesus says he is to fall into the hands of "the elders and chief priests and scribes, to be put to death," Peter jumps in to throw himself in the way. He will stop it even by force. Jesus tells him in no uncertain manner that anyone who uses force on his behalf is in the way. Such a one is in the way of God's plan.

If we are to be his followers we are to be just that—followers. Know your place, Peter, if you are behind me you are behind me. I am the way. You may not always understand the way but you have chosen it in choosing me. "If anyone wants to be a follower of mine, let him renounce himself and take up his cross and follow me." Sin can never achieve God's plan. That is the cross—we cannot do as we feel while disregarding the morality of our act. This is what renouncing ourselves means.

The wonder of this incident is that Peter remains Peter. He is still the Rock on which the Church will be built. But he is still on his journey. He is still to discover the meaning of "To be raised up on the third day." With his impetuosity, frailty and even sins, Jesus does not ever withdraw his promise.

Peter is like Jeremiah, "you have seduced me, my Lord, and I have let myself be seduced, you have overpowered me. You were the stronger. I am daily a laughing stock, everybody's butt." The prophet goes on to say he thought of giving up and not preaching the Lord. This would have been easier, because people did not understand. But "then there seemed to be a fire living in my heart." He could not forget the Lord—"I would not bear it." Peter sometimes did not understand, got it wrong, even denied the Lord, but with tears he returned. He could not bear the greatest loss of all—to be without his Lord. In the end he did take up his cross and follow to death—and to life.

Twenty-third Sunday Ordinary Time

Even with the rock foundation, the gift of the Holy Spirit and the assurance of the abiding presence of Jesus, the community he has called together still has its human problems.

Matthew here speaks out of experience. It is the experience of human shortcomings and the experience of being in touch with Jesus. The shortcomings will always be there but so, also, will be the solution for those who are open to the Spirit of Jesus.

We are called to have the moral courage to be truthful—to speak the truth and to live the truth.

Most of us, I am sure, have experienced, either personally, or through our friends, the hurt, misunderstanding and unresolved conflict caused by the judgments and condemnation of another. Often people judge, condemn and communicate their condemnation to others without even speaking to their accused victim.

Even if this is acceptable social behavior, it is not acceptable Christian behavior. Jesus calls his followers to a higher standard. He calls us to the love, understanding and forgiveness that his Spirit gives.

"If your brother does something wrong, go and have it out with him alone, between your two selves." What a beautiful, healthy, life-giving statement. But it takes courage. Speaking frankly to someone we care about contains the risk of our being rejected and hurt.

The cross that Jesus asks his followers to take up does not always imply the courage to face physical suffering. It is more often a call to moral courage. It is a call to live by his standards.

Unfortunately many people speak to their "brother" of his alleged wrongdoing at the wrong time and in the wrong spirit. It is not when the Holy Spirit moves to heal but when they are moved to hurt by the irrational spirits of temper or alcohol.

True Christian confrontation is done out of love, in times of calm and reason with a view to finding the truth, in openness to being mistaken oneself; tentatively, so that it is more of a question than an accusation.

In this way misunderstandings are a way to growth, to deeper knowledge of the other and deeper self-knowledge. There are different ways of feeling things, expressing ourselves and communicating.

When two are gathered in this spirit, Jesus is in the midst of them. When two get together in a genuine search for truth they are acting in the name, that is in the Spirit of Jesus. What they ask will be granted. They will find happiness.

If we followed the way of Jesus in this there would not be the devastating alienation that exists in society, from marriage breakdown to wars between whole communities.

As Christians we have a duty to help others grow in maturity and goodness. We have a responsibility to listen and allow others to speak to us with loving frankness.

The Church gives us the Gospel passage in the setting of the warning to Ezekiel, "If you . . . do not speak to warn the wicked man . . . I will hold you responsible . . ."

It is part of our Christian calling to be appropriately, wisely and gently critical and to accept helpful criticism with thanks. It is also important to give praise and encouragement and to accept praise realistically. The communication of truth and love give life. When these things are not accepted the flow of life ceases—there is no more communion. As Jesus puts it, "treat him like a pagan or a tax collector." It is more a sad reality than a condemnation. Jesus has been called the friend of the tax collectors and sinners. They may put themselves outside the community. His love is always there to welcome them back. So it should be with the gathering of believers that brings about his presence.

Twenty-fourth Sunday Ordinary Time

Last Sunday's Gospel called us to Christian confrontation. Jesus told those involved in difficulties and differences to face up to each other, then to be reconciled by seeking the truth together and asking and accepting forgiveness. We were left with the thought that forgiveness may not be offered or accepted. In this case the offending person unfortunately brings about separation and alienation. But for the follower of Jesus the door is never shut. As with the master, the disciples remain open to reconciliation. When Jesus says "treat him like a pagan or tax collector" (Mat. 18:17) we recall that he healed pagans and was called the friend of tax collectors. The author of this Gospel was a tax collector.

St Peter, with his newly promised power of binding and loosing, asks for a guiding law on forgiveness, "Lord, how often must I forgive my brother if he wrongs me?" He even offers a suggestion. "As often as seven times." A bit rash? But he knows Jesus is generous.

One of the basic changes which took place with the Second Vatican Council was the change in the accepted meaning of responsibility in the life of a Catholic.

Some years ago, after a talk on some of the implications of this, a member of the group asked a question along these lines:

"Has the Church gone soft? What has become of the strict demands of Lenten penance, the laws of fast and abstinence and other demanding Church laws that called for some discipline? People are doing nothing by way of penance these days."

Responsibility and discipline in the view of the questioner were measured by his response to the set of rules given from outside and clearly defined, even by weight, measure and time.

The Church now asks us to respond to a call for God, sought after through prayerful response to reality. There are the unforgiven, the alienated, the poor, the starving. People I know and people I will never know. What is my response as a child of God?—a realistic yet generous response. This is a different demand from the previous one. I suggest it is a much more self-disciplined and difficult one.

We see today something of this in the intention of Jesus. Peter wants a law for forgiveness. How many times before it is enough? How far must I go in order to avoid sin?

The response of Jesus is that it has nothing to do with time and amounts. It has all to do with attitude. We are made in God's image. We act like it. God is all-forgiving.

Easy? Improbable without the gift of the Holy Spirit—God's life within. Jesus asks us to respond to that creative life.

In the parable Jesus tells us the same thing that he places in his prayers: "Forgive us our trespasses, as we forgive those who trespass against us." One is impossible without the other because "Resentment and anger, they are foul things and both are found with the sinner" (Eccl. 27:30). We cannot be genuine in asking forgiveness while we are still sinning.

If you have not yet arrived, do not be discouraged. But do ask God gently and constantly to give you the freedom and happiness for the fullness of his Blessed Spirit—the Spirit of life, forgiveness and creation.

Twenty-fifth Sunday Ordinary Time

This is not a lesson on how to treat the staff, or on employer–employee relationships, enterprise bargaining, the necessity of trade unions. It is not in fact about people at work.

It is about the kingdom of heaven. It is about God and us. It is about the strange things God does—strange things like creating us, calling us to share his life, loving everyone. We were warned in this first reading, "Yes the heavens are as high above earth as my ways are above your ways, my thought above your thoughts."

We can waste our time judging, condemning and passing sentence on the worthiness of each other. We can waste time assessing our own worth.

A lovely lady once said to me, "I can see why my husband was created, he does so much good. But I don't know why God gave me life." Her husband's response was beautiful, affirming, practical and given out of love.

But really we do not have to justify our existence. God chose to create. He chose to create human life. I am a result of his creation. It is beyond me to know why God did these things. But we have the facts—we exist. We are not capable of assessing the work of God as though the creator were an exam assignment.

What God asks of us is that we come to know his love for us, and therefore respond with love. Further, through Jesus, he lets us know of the kingdom here, whose end will be the total and eternal union with the Absolute—total joy and fulfillment and love.

This parable of the people called by the landowner is about God's invitation into that kingdom: "The kingdom of heaven is like . . ." Who knows what we really achieve towards building that kingdom of love and justice and peace here? Who knows what anyone achieves in relation to working in the kingdom? These are things impossible to assess. Comparison is not only futile, it is destructive. We see this in the parable. God calls all. The task, the call, the details are insignificant in comparison with the fact that God calls all of us to share in his life and love.

The one thing necessary is that we constantly seek to deepen our understanding and acceptance of the fact of God's infinite, universal yet personal love. When his love lives in us we will wait for his call. We will be ready to say yes to the task. The time and the nature of the task we leave to God.

We do not have to look sideways at the other person's response or seeming lack of response. We are attentive to his call in the Word, in the events of life and in our own depths where he dwells. We may not know exactly what "You go into my vineyard" implies but we ask that we will be ready to say yes with gratitude and love.

Twenty-sixth Sunday Ordinary Time

The casual yes of the flippant son is not sufficient to sustain the perseverance and courage required for the day in the Father's vineyard—God's work. For that call by the Father to his children is an invitation into his life of loving creation. Christianity is an active response to that call. It is not merely something that is done to us as babies. Without our response it is meaningless.

We see in the story that God is patient in waiting for the response. But he accepts it when it is a yes with meaning.

Surely the attitude of both sons can be identified in most of us as we are called day by day to respond with meaning and love. Sometimes we surprise ourselves with our generosity. Sometimes we do not live up to the original intention. Then, at times, we disappoint ourselves with negative attitudes only to think it over and repair the damage with greater love and concern. "I wish I had not felt that way, said that, done that. I should have been more generous, more listening, more caring."

It is precisely at this point that we again begin to say yes as the son in the Gospel did—with meaning.

It is important to remember that we are not responsible for our feelings anyway. People often express guilt for having felt anger or hurt. Feelings are automatic. The feeling we have is a fact that we must admit and deal with as we should with any other significant fact. It is what we do with the feeling that constitutes our yes or no to the Father's call. It is here that we can decide to seek revenge or to seek understanding and reconciliation. Perhaps we will not immediately make the positive response, but we can work towards it.

We easily say "Amen"—"Yes, Father" to *The Lord's Prayer*. Would a more authentic response sometimes be, "I will think about it"? Thy will be done, sharing our daily bread, forgiving as God forgives. A glib "Amen" and then go off to do as we wish, or a deep consideration, change and action? Yes I will go into the vineyard of my heart and mind and soul and work towards the things my Father calls me to do.

Twenty-seventh Sunday Ordinary Time

The people to whom Jesus is speaking here know very well, "Yes the vineyard of the Lord of hosts is the House of Israel and the men of Judah the chosen plant."

Yet he has the courage to tell them this parable, warning them of the way in which they are heading—"The kingdom will be taken away from you and given to a people who will produce fruit." These are dangerous words when spoken to chief priests and elders.

But Jesus must be true to his Father. His love has expressed itself in acts of gentle healing, loving forgiveness and encouraging words, and here, in harsh words of warning.

He is practicing what he preached. "If your brother does something wrong go and have it out with him" (Matt 18:15).

The terrible wrong that wounds the loving heart of Jesus is that those in power, in possession of the kingdom, the ones to whom the vineyard is entrusted, have betrayed that trust.

Any power we have is "leased to the tenants," until the master returns. The gift of any talents or position or any of privilege or power if we are truly workers in the Lord's vineyard is given for all. The unfortunate chief priests and elders had used these things to increase themselves while the people they were meant to serve remained their ignorant servants. "Woe to you lawyers also! You lay impossible burdens on men but will not lift a finger to lighten them" (Luke 12:47).

"Woe to you lawyers! You have taken away the key of knowledge. You yourselves have not gained access, yet you have stopped those who wished to enter" (Luke 12:52).

The parable is a story of one who receives gifts on trust for the good of the kingdom and grows rich on them himself. This means that the servants who come to collect the gifts are expendable. They are thrashed and stoned and killed. Even the son is expendable if he stands in the way of their proud will. How often the story has been repeated and continues to be acted out today.

The use of God's gifts, whatever they may be, to destroy, degrade and make mere use of other people is a terrible insult to the divine generosity and trust.

Again and again those in possession of power or property or talents of any kind need to meditate on this parable. And those people and organizations are all of us.

May the master speak to our hearts and let us know that we are ministers and tenants of his gifts and property. May he give us the wisdom and spirit of poverty to act always in a creative way—for we carry the seed of his creative being within us.

Twenty-eighth Sunday Ordinary Time

"Many are called but few are chosen." We who have come here to worship God and pray for all can hardly be unmoved by these words. Jesus does not speak idle or meaningless words. Isn't this a sad summary of the story of God's invitation sent out to all? St Paul puts it in unmistakable words: "God . . . wants all to be saved and to come to know the truth" (1 Tim 2:4).

The story told by Jesus is of this universal love of God. Invitations go in all directions without any discrimination at all. As the story develops we see that few are chosen because few accept the gracious invitation. God chooses all, the rest is up to us. We then may choose to say yes, or we may turn the other way. Love cannot force. The terms "love and force" are incompatible.

The difficulty comes when we are confronted with what our yes to God implies. Acceptance to enjoy the delights of God's banquet implies acceptance of allowing others to live fully and enjoy the gifts of God. It implies a maturity that few seemed to have reached.

Maturity implies the willingness to put off a present good, or supposed good, for a future greater good. The people in the story are no different from people in every age and in every place. Few seem to see beyond their own present needs, demands and satisfactions.

There is nothing wrong with the farm or the business, to use the examples of the story, but there is certainly more to life than my own material concerns here and now—farm or business or whatever they are.

When the whole picture is ignored, then even the farm and the business can become sources of evil. We only have to look at the destruction of God's beautiful earth, the dispossession of indigenous peoples, the greed of the unrestrained ego and the hatred cultivated by those who want to keep their power and wealth while others remain dispossessed and starving, to see that few have chosen God's way of being loving and creative sharers.

If we human beings had accepted God's invitation to the wedding of God with humanity in Christ, we would have a loving, creative world. Since we, on the whole, have not, the world is a place where self-interest has resulted in the tragedies we continue to inflict on each other. God continues to invite us to more, much more than this. It can only come about by our accepting the invitation to celebrate and live universal love and unselfish sharing.

A formal, ritualistic religion produces nothing. The man without the wedding garment was there physically, but his heart was far from there. St Paul speaks of putting on Christ, having the same mind as Christ. This is what I mean. This is precisely why, by the very nature of things that man has excluded himself. His body was there, his mind had never changed.

We can only hope, pray and work that eventually in some way, God's children will see the wonder of unselfish love so that all will know the warm welcome and loving embrace of the Absolute. Here and now let us enter this banquet with enthusiastic joy and gratitude.

Twenty-ninth Sunday Ordinary Time

"Give back to Caesar what belongs to Caesar—and to God what belongs to God."

Those words have been used to excuse all sorts of injustices done in the name of giving to Caesar what is Caesar's. People have justified obeying unjust laws, going to wars of oppression and "being loyal" to systems and people who deserve no loyalty.

What belongs to Caesar, the unjust oppressor, is nothing. Jesus is not making any political statement here, he is treating their vindictive malice with the contempt it deserves.

It is significant that here is the old story of politics, whether it is the politics of a small group or politics on a national or international scale. Enemies unite when they oppose a common enemy. Principles often suffer in the union. But winning is the objective. The Pharisees observed the law in a strict, legalistic way. They could not tolerate the Roman oppressor or anything to do with Caesar. The Herodians supported the occupying forces. Yet they are willing to come together to oppose goodness when it seems to question their positions of power. They, not he, are the ones who have their beloved "money you pay the tax with" ready at hand. He sends them off to play with their beloved money and power.

He has no message for them because they have not come to learn by asking questions, but to set him up for further criticism. He has no hesitation in calling them hypocrites.

It is a bit like the media show that invites a discussion on the Church only to set its teaching up for misunderstanding, ridicule and entertainment. How many "inquiries" of the media are a real search for the truth? How many are entertainment for ratings? We keep hoping they are genuine searches for truth.

What is the positive message here for those who want to learn?

"Give to God what belongs to God."

Doesn't everything belong to God? "To God belongs the earth and all it contains, the world and all who live there" (PS 24:1) were words Jesus knew by heart and prayed with his people. The only thing that belongs to anyone else is the misuse of the beauty God had entrusted to us as stewards. We call this misuse "sin."

Waste, destruction, oppression of others, unjust use of power or force, money or position. Let Caesar have these. Give them back, throw them away. Give glory to God, as St Paul taught us, "Whatever you eat, whatever you drink, whatever you do at all, do it for the glory of God" (1 Cor 10:31). The use of God's gifts with gratitude and with respect for the rights, freedom and needs of others is giving to God what is God's. Then we raise his creation up in an act of thanksgiving and let it lead us and others to the fulfillment of our potential as images of God himself. Then, like Jesus, we give glory to God by the very fact of our existence.

Thirtieth Sunday Ordinary Time

The absolute love and a lovableness of God does not consist of anything God does in creation. Love is what God is. His external acts are a result of this love that is.

This is why Jesus answers the question about the greatest commandment in this way, "You shall love." It is not in doing or avoiding specific things that greatness, goodness and beauty of life consists, but in the quality of love that motivates life and its consequent activity. The attitude from which all our actions spring will determine the quality of those actions.

Since we are made in God's image, the answer to life consists in living and reflecting his creative love. The Godlike person can never be destructive. All sin is destructive in some way.

Fully mature Christians, Christ-like people, need no commandments. Their activity, springing from love, does not need direction from outside. They are inner-directed towards goodness. As with any finite creature they need knowledge and help in discerning the true good. In difficult circumstances they need the help of other wise and good people in reaching a conclusion as to what seems best. Their search will be unselfish and honest. Their response will be willing.

As to laws and regulations about how much or how little, these have come into existence precisely because generosity has been wanting and immaturity seeks the easiest way out.

Immaturity asks what must I do to avoid trouble. Goodness and maturity asks what can I do to bring happiness.

Imagine a community of mature, loving Christians. They would not need laws to tell them to worship the God they love with their whole heart and soul and mind. It would not be necessary to say "Honor your father and mother" or "parents, live in such a way to deserve this honor." The gifts of love and sex and good name and property would be respected because the violation of these could never spring from love.

In such an ideal society the only laws necessary would be common agreements for the free flow of society; for example, rules for use of the roads, times to meet for worship, work, play or hospitality.

It is clear that law comes into the world through selfishness and sin. In our own society we see laws being multiplied. As selfish and greedy people find a way around a law, another is enacted to cover the loophole. And it goes on, as it seems endlessly. Sin and selfishness enslave. True, unselfish love liberates. A truly moral life brings happiness.

To live in generous response to the great commandment we need the wisdom, insight and spiritual energy that comes only from God. We need to take every opportunity to open our lives to his dynamic love.

Thirty-first Sunday Ordinary Time

During the ordination of a deacon the bishop hands the newly ordained the book and says, "Receive the Gospel of Christ whose herald you now are. Believe what you read, teach what you believe and practice what you teach." The rite has reminded the man that he is to imitate Christ, who came, not to be served but to serve.

The very word minister means one who serves. In the Gospel today Jesus reminds us of the qualities of Christian leadership: "The greatest among you must be your servant."

In the truly Christian community, whatever the size, home, parish or diocese, individual gifts are not received for personal glorification. Whether these are gifts of mind, body, parenthood, ministry, appointed leadership, gifts of nature or gifts of portion, they are meant to be received graciously and gratefully and used with generosity and humility.

Jesus is grieved by the Pharisees, who have received the gift of learning and the call to leadership and use these things not to serve, but to keep others in their service. He knows very well how important example is. Yet he asks his true followers to see beyond the bad example even of people in authority.

There are people called rabbi, father, teacher. They should be these things in what they say and what they do. This, unfortunately, is not always the case. Jesus reminds his followers that in fact there is only one true Master, Father,

Teacher. Even if we are scandalized by those who are supposed to image the Master, Father, Teacher who is in heaven, please do remember that he can be betrayed by those whom he has entrusted with his love. He, however, will never betray.

True imagery of the Father, true leadership of any kind, is a leadership that is what it teaches, as Jesus was. The true leader in a small or large community never stands in the way of goodness, progress or the development of brothers and sisters. He and she are there to inspire, to encourage to help discern the good of the other. They are there to listen, to call those qualities forth, to appreciate and love the qualities in another. Jealousy and competition have no place in such a style of leadership. If someone does something better, is more qualified, has greater gifts, then thanks be to God for those gifts.

In such a realistic attitude as this true humility exists. Not only will this greatness be recognized but the whole community will be exalted by humble leadership. We all have some leadership role. We all can be inspirational encouragers, sensitive listeners and faithful images of what we believe.

Thirty-second Sunday Ordinary Time

The liturgy of the word calls us to consider wisdom and foolishness and to consider these things in relation to the kingdom of heaven.

The Book of Wisdom tells in poetic language of God's longing to impart his gift of wisdom. "She herself walks about looking for those who are worthy of her and graciously shows herself to them as they go, in every thought of theirs coming to meet them." Jesus has assured us, "If you, with all your sins, know how to give your children good things, how much more will the heavenly Father give the Holy Spirit to those who ask him" (Luke 11:8). Yes we can have divine wisdom if the desire is there, if the mind is open and the prayer sincere. But because wisdom is a divine gift, we receive it in the measure that we are willing to make way for it. This requires letting go of pettiness. The foolish bridesmaids were mean in their preparation for the bridegroom, the wise ones wholehearted.

The wise person has the ability to see things in their true perspective and to respond in the appropriate way. We have experience of foolish people who will treat a small, insignificant incident as though their eternal destiny depended on it. Yet things of importance receive scant consideration.

The parable tells the story of a wedding preparation, but it is about the kingdom of God. It is about how seriously we treat the reality of God's call to his kingdom here and his invitation to the eternal wedding—perfect union with him forever.

Shining, beautiful lamps, carried by beautifully dressed and presented people, but with nothing inside them, will never light the darkness. Jesus calls us to be people of substance who are filled with the holy oil of his wisdom and understanding. He asks us to be light to the world as he is light to the world. No matter how long he is in coming, either in our individual lives or in the final call of all things to himself, he still calls listening, loving people to carry his divine gift.

It is not in any sense of tension or fear that these wise ones wait but in joyful expectation. Then whether Jesus comes today in the person of one in need or one with encouragement or truth or a challenge to greater goodness, they will recognize him. His coming is today, this week, in so many ways, as surely as it will be when he is no longer seen through the veil but seen face to face.

Thirty-third Sunday Ordinary Time

Christians should be well aware, from listening to the Gospel, that they are called by God, graced by God and invited to respond.

The kingdom is like a man who (1) summoned his servants, (2) entrusted them with his property and (3) left them to it.

There is no question about competition or relative importance, just the need to respond. There is a big risk in entrusting the gifts of the kingdom to mere servants. Surely this is an act of extraordinary, loving trust. Such precious gifts are not entrusted merely to be preserved like some precious family treasure in a bank vault. "I have it and I will hold onto it and I will never take the risk of disturbing it" is not the message of the Gospel. Neither is receiving the gift and merely leaving it there.

These attitudes, I suggest, are precisely the attitudes that lead to "even what he has will be taken away." Haven't we all experienced what is called the loss of faith in people who could have responded to the crisis in faith by investing all they had. Every one of our crisis times in life can be the point at which we give up hope and bury the gift or the point at which the very crisis itself calls us to greater depths of faith.

This doubling of talents can take place when we have the courage to accept whatever reality is present, the courage to admit our weakness, our mistakes, our sin, if that is there; the courage to admit our need of God and of other human beings, the courage to share with others what we feel, our confusion, doubt, fear. These times of crisis may be merely the process of growing up. It is sad that so many miss the precious opportunity to really grow.

As the parable implies, growth in faith, in the kingdom, implies doing as God did. We are asked to trust one another, to take the risk of investing what God has given us.

What is true of the individual Christian is true of the Church on every level. The home, the parish, the diocese, the universal Church will only grow if we are prepared to take the risk of trusting each other. The gifts are there to be shared and thus to increase.

The Church is called, not merely to preserve the faith, certainly not to bury it in case someone tampers with it. We are called to share it, to listen to every culture and time and philosophy and to interact. The risk of the search, of the investment in ideas, of the development of theology, pastoral initiatives, justice issues will return a hundredfold. Preserving, prohibiting, restricting, reacting with fear for change are not for people of faith. The search in awe, wonder, question, hope in the Spirit are not for the timid, lazy servant. These are things of the kingdom.

Last Sunday Ordinary Time— The Feast of Christ the King

This is an immense picture painted in a few words. "When the Son of Man comes in his glory" brings to our minds the wrapping up of all things in Christ and their glorified beauty, in him, presented to the Father.

Here he tells us what brings the glory and the beauty of divine life to human life. But all through his teaching he has told us this: "Lord, which is the greatest of the commandments?" Which, of all the "thou shalt nots," is the most important? Jesus leaves the negatives and stresses the one thing necessary for union with God. It is not refraining from something but doing and being something: "Thou shall love."

Even reading today's Gospel passage we may ask ourselves, "When did I last give a hungry person food, a thirsty, drink, a naked, clothes, or visit the sick; have I ever even been in a prison?"

We hope we can all say something like "only yesterday" to some to these questions. But even that is not the point. How would a Trappist Monk or a Carmelite nun or the bishops and cardinals of the Roman Curia answer these questions? No. The point again is love. Can I see suffering and distress and not be moved to suffer with my brothers and sisters? Do I really love God, who created every one of us, with all my heart, and so love his children? The one who thus loves must take some action. This loving relationship with God can never be satisfied by "what rules must I keep?"

There is only one thing necessary for my union with God, for the ultimate vision, possession and delight of his presence. It is the same thing that makes me delighted to be in the presence of anyone. If it is missing I can't bear being there for long—certainly not for eternity. It is, of course, love.

Performing duties, even the ones Jesus talks about here, is not the essence. Love is the essence, the deeds are the inevitable result. These deeds are not grace, the gift of God's Spirit, but the result of grace. When God and the human soul are one, Godlike deeds follow.

Writing on the final words of the *Creed*, "life everlasting, Amen," after speaking of our joy in God, St Thomas Aquinas says, "Finally, eternal life consists in the joyful companionship of all the blessed, a companionship which is full of delight; since each one will possess all good things together with all the blessed, for they will all love one another as themselves, and therefore, will rejoice in one another's happiness as if it were their own, and consequently the joy and gladness of one will be as great as the joy of all."

Love is not an optional extra. It is the essence of union with God.